PHOENIX FROM THE ASHES?

PHOENIX FROM THE ASHES?

Russia's Defence Industrial Complex
and its Arms Exports

Cameron Scott Mitchell

THE AUSTRALIAN NATIONAL UNIVERSITY

E PRESS

E PRESS

Published by ANU E Press
The Australian National University
Canberra ACT 0200, Australia
Email: anuepress@anu.edu.au
This title is also available online at: http://epress.anu.edu.au/phoenix_citation.html

National Library of Australia
Cataloguing-in-Publication entry

Author: Mitchell, Cameron.
Title: Phoenix from the ashes? : Russia's defence industrial complex
               and its arms exports / Cameron Mitchell.
ISBN: 9781921666117 (pdf) 9781921666100 (pbk.)
Series: Canberra papers on strategy and defence ; 175.
Notes: Bibliography.
Subjects: Weapons industry—Russia.
               Russia—Social conditions.
               Russia—Economic aspects.
               Russia—Economic condition.
Dewey Number: 338.4762340947

The *Canberra Papers on Strategy and Defence* series is a collection of publications arising principally from research undertaken at the SDSC. Canberra Papers have been peer reviewed since 2006. All Canberra Papers are available for sale: visit the SDSC website at <http://rspas.anu.edu.au/sdsc/canberra_papers.php> for abstracts and prices. Electronic copies (in pdf format) of most SDSC Working Papers published since 2002 may be downloaded for free from the SDSC website at <http://rspas.anu.edu.au/sdsc/working_papers.php>. The entire Working Papers series is also available on a 'print on demand' basis.

Cover design by ANU E Press

Table of Contents

Synopsis

The continued existence of the Russian defence and arms industry, known as the *Oboronnyi-promyshennyi kompleks* (OPK), was called into question following the disintegration of the Soviet Union in 1991. Industry experts cited the lack of a domestic market, endemic corruption, and excess capacity within the industry as factors underpinning its predicted demise. The most telling factor was the sudden removal of considerable government subsidies and high defence industry wages that had traditionally buttressed the industry's economic viability and encouraged the cream of Russia's workers into the sector. It was a crippling blow. However, the industry's export customers in China, India and Iran during those early years became the OPK's saving grace. Their orders introduced hard currency back into the industry and went a long way to preventing the forecasted OPK collapse. Although pessimistic predictions continued to plague the OPK throughout the 1990s, the valuable export dollars provided the OPK the breathing space it needed to claw back its competitive advantage as an arms producer. That revival has been further underpinned by a new political commitment, various research and development initiatives, and the restoration of defence industry as a tool of Russian foreign policy.

In order to gauge the future prospects for the OPK, it is necessary to examine the domestic and external drivers that have either underwritten its success to date or are still required to ensure its long-term endurance. Domestically, continued success demands a closer collaboration between the OPK and the Russian armed forces. It also requires serious efforts to curb endemic corruption, further consolidation of the defence industry, and continued development of the Russian domestic market for arms. Externally, the strength of the state arms exporter, Rosoboronexport, global market diversification and joint military ventures with strategic partner countries are essential ingredients for long-term OPK success. Cultivating and maintaining the economic and political momentum vital for the OPK's progress will be a daunting undertaking for Russia. However, Russia's accomplishments in these key areas since 2000 suggest that continued success is a genuine prospect and that the OPK could potentially grow to be the proverbial 'phoenix from the ashes'.

China and India constitute approximately 60 per cent of the total Russian arms transfer market. Trading and cooperation with these two countries has provided Moscow with the finances to sustain its defence industry through continued orders and valuable finance for research and development programs for military hardware. However, post 2012, the Chinese market will be nearing total saturation and the Indian market will have contracted somewhat, as the indigenous defence industries of these nations can be expected to usurp the demand for Russian equipment. This scenario, together with a more active foreign policy under Vladimir Putin has seen Russia launch aggressive marketing campaigns into the Middle East, Southeast Asia and Latin America. The strategy has already begun to pay dividends, with multi-billion dollar contracts being signed by Algeria, Indonesia, Venezuela, and possibly Libya. The Russians hope that large sales to these countries will trigger further sales within the respective regions. The realised or potential contracts for arms from Saudi Arabia, Malaysia, Mexico, and Brazil suggest that this strategy is producing the desired result.

The short-term future of the Russian OPK looks promising. The rising domestic defence order is beginning to challenge the export market as the OPK's most important customer. Meanwhile, exports will be safeguarded by continued foreign demand for niche Russian defence products such as cruise missiles and air-defence systems, as well as cost effective and user friendly Russian aircraft, ships, submarines and land systems. Flexible financing options offered by Rosoboronexport will stimulate demand in new or renewed markets such as Algeria and Indonesia and sustain the economic viability of the OPK for at least the next decade.

Although the long-term future of the OPK is more difficult to predict, Russia's solid research and development foundation and successful international joint military ventures suggest that the current thriving trend in exports is likely to continue. To preserve traditional markets, Russia will, over time, probably permit greater technology transfer and perhaps even shift its exports to higher-end niche military equipment. Russia represents the next generation of affordable and rugged military equipment for the arsenals of the developing world. Coupled with Russia's growing ability to rearm itself through rising oil prices and a more streamlined defence industry, the future of the OPK looks bright.

*   *   *

Disclaimer

The opinions and views expressed in this paper are those of the author alone and do not reflect in any way those of the Australian Department of Defence. In addition, all data included in this paper is available from open source materials.

About the Author

Cameron Scott Mitchell has a career background in Defence Intelligence. He has worked on a range of Defence related strategic issues, and deployed to Iraq as a Senior Intelligence Officer working in the Combined Intelligence Operation Centre in 2007. He holds an honours degree in history from the University of Sydney, and graduated with a Masters degree by research from the University of New South Wales. His academic focus includes Russian and Chinese military modernisation and defence reform. He has been published in *Strategic Comments*, through the International Institute for Strategic Studies.

Acknowledgements

I wish to thank Alex Brooking, Alexandra Siddall and the staff at the Australian embassy in Moscow for their time and assistance with interviews and collating information.

Oksana Antonenko at the International Institute for Strategic Studies in London, Pavel Felgenhauer, an independent Russian Defence Analyst in Moscow, and Ruslan Pukhov at the Centre for Analysis of Strategies and Technologies, also in Moscow, granted me interviews, while Ruslan also showed continued interest and gave further assistance.

I am grateful to my immediate family, including my wife Sophie, who pushed me and were patient with me. Proofreading and input by friends David Hirst and Tegan Smith were also invaluable, as was the support of other friends and family, including Pru and Rob Howse, and Eric and Diana Mitchell.

Finally, I extend gratitude to Professor Stewart Woodman for his supervision and valuable contributions, which added much needed structure and further argument to the paper.

Acronyms and Abbreviations

ADS	Air-Defence Ship
APC	Armoured Personnel Carrier
ASCM	Anti-Ship Cruise Missile
ASEAN	Association of Southeast Asian Nations
CIS	Commonwealth of Independent States
DIA	Defense Intelligence Agency
EADS	European Aeronautic Defence and Space Company
EU	European Union
GDP	Gross Domestic Product
ICBM	Inter-continental ballistic missile
IFV	Infantry Fighting Vehicle
MANPAD	Man Portable Air Defence System
MIC	Military Industrial Commission
MiG-AT	MiG Advanced Trainer
MBT	Main Battle Tank
MoD	Ministry of Defence
MoU	Memorandum of Understanding
MTA	Medium Transport Aircraft
OAK	*Obdinyonnaya Aviasroitelnaya Korporatsiya* (Unified Aircraft Corporation)
OPK	*Oboronnyi-promyshennyi kompleks*
PLA	People's Liberation Army
R&D	Research and Development
SAM	surface-to-air missile
SCO	Shanghai Cooperation Organisation

SDO	State Defence Order
STOVL	short takeoff/vertical landing
TVT	thrust-vector technology
UAE	United Arab Emirates
VPK	*Voennyi-promyshlennyi kompleks*

List of Figures and Tables

Chapter 1
Phoenix from the Ashes?

As Russia gains economic strength, it will be capable of more assertive postures in many areas. Barring a radical reversal of current trends, post-Soviet Russia will in the next few years have many options it has not yet had in its brief existence as a nation—options in international relations vis-à-vis the developed West, the third world, and, most immediately, its neighbours from the former Soviet Union. An economically stronger Russia will also be able to spend more on its defence.

Clifford Gaddy[1]

Russia's defense industrial complex, or *Oboronnyi-promyshennyi kompleks* (OPK), has endured much over the past 15 years. Originally known as the military industrial complex (VPK), it became known as the OPK in the late 1990s. The political, social and economic transition from Soviet Union to Russian Federation was far from smooth, and the upheaval surrounding this political reversal manifested itself within the OPK. The rampant corruption and general disintegration of state systems witnessed during the death throes of the Soviet Union and the early years of the Russian Federation was no more evident anywhere than in the OPK.

At the end of the 1980s, the Soviet Union's VPK consisted of approximately 4000 research institutions, design organisations and production facilities. These state enterprises always received the lion's share of talent, technology and funding from the state, which unofficially devoted nearly 50 per cent of a central government budget of well over US$80 billion to military expenditures.[2] Many cities such as Sverdlovsk (now Yekaterinburg) and Nizhny Tagil were massive defence plants, with almost all of the population involved in defence industry. They lived in company apartments, shopped in company stores and ate in company cafes. Up to 80 per cent of a defence plant's budget went to maintaining these social services;[3] all of which fell under the sweeping term 'Defence' within the Soviet budget. These examples highlight the importance of state funding to the survival of the VPK. It therefore came as no surprise

1   Clifford Gaddy, 'No Turning Back: Market Reform and Defense Industry in Russia: Who's adjusting to whom?', Brookings Institution, Washington, DC, Summer 1996, available at <http://www.brookings.edu/ articles/1996/summer_russia_gaddy.aspx>, accessed 28 April 2009.

2   Anthony H. Cordesman, *The Strategic Impact of Russian Arms Sales and Technology Transfers*, Center for Strategic and International Studies, Washington, DC, 5 April 1999, pp. 10–11, available at <http://www.csis. org/media/csis/pubs/atstratimpofrussarmsale%5B1%5D.pdf>, accessed 28 April 2009.

3   See 'Military Industry Overview', GlobalSecurity.org, available at <www.globalsecurity.org/military/ world/russia/industry-overview.htm>, accessed 28 April 2009.

that the VPK suffered greatly during the early and mid-1990s (especially during the 1998 economic crisis), when the newly formed Russian Federation could do little to stop the decay of an industry traditionally reliant upon state direction and funding. Defence budgets of the new Russia were low on the agenda of a Yeltsin Administration facing considerable social upheaval, and hence they equated to a fraction of the mammoth amounts of their Communist forebears.

The Communist-era VPK was organised within an authoritarian political system that devoted vast amounts of resources and funding to the defence sector. The experiences of the Great Patriotic War, nationalism, and Communist ideology provided the background for a national security strategy focused purely on combating capitalism, chiefly in the form of the United States. This undertaking demanded a large defence force and extensive military production to keep pace with military developments in the West. Russia's educated population and extensive mineral resource reserves facilitated this.[4] The economic growth rate slackened in the late 1970s, leading to an increase in the share of defence spending within the Soviet economy. Coupled with this development was the fact that Soviet military technology at the 'high end' did not match Western technology. To combat this, Soviet military planners countered Western technology with Soviet quantity in the form of 'middle technology' weapon systems.[5] The crippling costs associated with matching US military technological might with Soviet numerical might led to the eventual collapse of the Soviet Union, despite Mikhail Gorbachev's last-ditch attempts to reduce defence spending.[6]

Faced with political and social upheaval, and a dramatic reduction in the resource base during the 1990s, military exports—or arms transfers—became the saving grace of many enterprises within the VPK. With little or no domestic demand for arms, and vast amounts of half-finished weapon systems sitting in the factories, Russian defence companies looked elsewhere, and found eager buyers in China, India, and Iran. Valuable hard currency began to trickle in, after bribes had been paid to officials from the countries receiving the weaponry, and corrupt Russian officials had taken their cut. This precious currency prolonged the survival of some of Russia's more successful defence enterprises, but was by no means enough to sustain the industry as a whole. It was during this period that pessimistic opinions emerged as to the future of the VPK. Experts, such as Vitaly Shlykov, an ex-member of the Soviet Ministry of Defence, and Stephen Blank, a respected US-based analyst, predicted an eventual collapse of the VPK.

---

4   Paul Rivlin, *The Russian Economy and Arms Exports to the Middle East,* Memorandum no. 79, The Jaffee Centre for Strategic Studies, Tel Aviv University, November 2005, p. 14, available at <http://www.inss.org.il/upload/(FILE)1188301974.pdf>, accessed 28 April 2009.

5   Rivlin, *The Russian Economy and Arms Exports to the Middle East,* p. 14.

6   Edward A. Corcoran, *Perestroika and the Soviet Military: Implications for US Policy,* Cato Policy Analysis no. 133, 29 May 1990, available at <http://www.cato.org/pubs/pas/pa133.html>, accessed 28 April 2009.

Moreover, the respected Moscow-based defence analyst Pavel Felgenhauer made a statement in 2002 canvassing Russia's ability to produce conventional submarines:

> The 'Krasnoye Sormovo' shipyard in Nizhny Novgorod no longer makes Kilo submarines after building the last two for China. Admiralteyskaya Verf in St. Petersburg is also now only renovating Kilos made for India in the 1980s. Specialists say Russia cannot make a single Kilo anymore.[7]

The predicted collapse of the VPK would result from a combination of endemic corruption, insufficient government funding, a 'brain-drain' to the lucrative defence industries in the West, and the devastating effects of neglecting long-term research and development (R&D) programs.[8] These problems were particularly acute after 1993, when the vast bulk of the half-finished weapons had finally found customers and the various defence enterprises actually had to build equipment from scratch.

However, despite the turmoil of the last 15 years, and many pessimistic predictions, the VPK (also known as the OPK since late 1990s) still has the ability to produce air, land and naval equipment—an indication of the industry's resilience. In stark contradiction to Felgenhauer's comment, Russia signed a multi-billion dollar contract with China for the construction of eight Project 636 *Kilo*-class submarines on 3 May 2002. One of these submarines was successfully constructed in the shipyard at Nizhny Novgorod,[9] and five others at the Admiralty shipyards in St. Petersburg. All eight have subsequently been completed and delivered to China. This is one of a number of examples highlighting the resilience of the industry—a resilience that continues to confound the more pessimistic of the Russian defence industry analysts.

Gloomy predictions for the OPK's future were still being voiced in 2006; however the current environment is a vastly different one from that of the 1990s. The trajectory of the Russian defence industry was marked by a precipitous decline in the early and mid-1990s, bottoming out in 1997, but was then succeeded from 1998 by a rapid recovery—a 37 per cent rise in output in 1999, then a 25 per cent increase in 2000.[10] Output has increased annually since 2000, sitting

---

7   Pavel Felgenhauer, 'Arms Exports and the Russian Military', *Perspective*, vol. XII, no. 4, March–April 2002, p. 3, also available at <http://www.bu.edu/iscip/vol12/felgenhauer2.html>, accessed 28 April 2009.

8   Vitaly V. Shlykov in Steven E. Miller, and Dmitri V. Trenin (eds), *The Russian Military: Power and Policy*, MIT Press, Cambridge, MA, 2004; and Stephen J. Blank, *Reform and the Revolution in Russian Defense Economics*, Strategic Studies Institute, US Army War College, Carlisle, PA, 19 May 1995, available at <http://www.strategicstudiesinstitute.army.mil/pdffiles/PUB166.pdf>, accessed 28 April 2009.

9   Alexandra Gritskova, Konstantin Lantratov and Mikhail Barabanov, 'Russia Builds Chinese Navy', *Kommersant*, 22 December 2005, available at <http://www.kommersant.com/p637658/r_1/Russia_Builds_Chinese_Navy/>, accessed 28 April 2009.

10   Alexei Izyumov, Leonid Kosals, Rosalina Ryvkina and Yuri Semagin, 'Market Reforms and Regional Differentiation of Russia Defence Industry Enterprises', *Europe-Asia Studies*, vol. 54, no. 6, September 2002,

at around 16 per cent, although recent increases in domestic funding and multi-billion dollar arms export deals with Algeria, India and Venezuela in 2006, and probably Libya in 2007, could see output jump even higher. Even without taking future improvement into account, there is considerable evidence that the Russian defence sector is thriving thanks to its ability to transform itself through spin-offs and selective market developments. David Dyker's study of Russian economics indicated that the military was ahead of other science and technology sectors in realising the utility of dual-use technologies as well as in acknowledging that R&D should be client-driven.[11] To date, this trend has been the norm, with advanced technologies such as the Sukhoi Su-30MKI *Flanker* being sold to India and the Project 877/636 *Kilo*–class submarine/*Klub* (SS-N-27) missile system combination being sold to both India and China. In fact, by far the biggest influence on the success of the OPK since 2000 has been the boom in its exports. Russian arms exports have grown tremendously—from US$1.1 billion in 1992 to a post Soviet peak in 2008 of US$8 billion, and are now the OPKs main source of revenue. As one Ministry of Industry and Energy official put it: 'The OPK cannot survive with funds allocated by the government in the Defense Ministry's budget.'[12]

The defence industry is one of the few sectors in which Russia can successfully compete in international markets. The quality of Russian weapons is close to the standard of the best Western producers according to independent industry sources (a legacy of the importance placed on military R&D in the Soviet era) and at a price that is at least 30–35 per cent lower.[13] Russia's export potential in the short-term is strong: the total order book approximately equates to US$20 billion as at January 2009.[14]

Arms transfers have reached record levels since 1991, with 2008 figures estimated at US$8 billion.[15] Granted, this pales in significance to the levels reached by the Soviet Union; however, Soviet-era sales were rarely recompensed with hard currency. Moreover, the aim of this thesis is not to compare the two entities. It will be a long time, if ever, before Russian arms production and export levels match the levels achieved by the Soviet Union.

To make such a comparison, particularly as an omen for Russian defence industry failure, would be to misunderstand the nature of the new industrial

---

pp. 959–74 (960), available at <http://www.jstor.org/stable/826290>, accessed 28 April 2009.

11   Richard Cooper, 'Russia's Economy—The Best Case', in *Putin's Russia—Scenarios for 2005*, Jane's Information Group, Coulsdon, Surrey, 2004, p. 8.

12   Yuri Koptev, in 'Experts Concerned over Russia's Military-Industrial Complex', *RIA Novosti*, 11 November 2005, available at <http://en.rian.ru>, accessed 5 February 2006.

13   Benjamin Mahmud, 'Russian Defence Industry', *Asian Defence Journal*, October 2005, p. 39.

14   'Defence Production and R&D', *Jane's Sentinel Security Assessment: Russia*, Jane's Information Group, Coulsdon, Surrey, April 2009.

15   'Russian Federation—Defence Industry', *Jane's World Defence Industry*, Jane's Information Group, Coulsdon, Surrey, 2006, 19 January 2009.

and export environment. Russia now competes for military exports not only with Europe and the United States, but also Belarus, the Ukraine, and other states that made up the former Soviet Union. Therefore, a more reasoned approach to assessing Russian military output is to compare the Russian OPK with its current competitors in Europe, the United States and Asia. This comparison will draw more reliable conclusions and provides more credible analysis of the OPKs current position.

Today, Russian sales have risen annually within a flat global market, with advanced aircraft, air-defence systems and utility helicopters the most popular exports. Even the naval industry, for so long the recipient of the most pessimistic survivability predictions, has begun to produce new-build submarines and ships rather than refurbished Soviet stock for delivery to China, India and Vietnam. Analysis of Russian arms transfers for 2005 indicates that naval equipment provided over 40 per cent of the earnings and that it was the primary revenue earner for the first time in several years. This being said, air defence systems returned to the top earnings place in 2006.[16] The competition between sectors for the top place each year is a good sign for the defence industry overall, which has experienced 14 per cent annual growth since 2000.

So significant has been the impact of exports on the new OPK that its major clients are the armed forces of other countries, as opposed to the Russian Federation armed forces. Russia's OPK is the only national defence industry in the world where exports account for more revenue than domestic orders. This has been a trend since 1991 and has led to some defence industrial R&D and production program (such as India's Sukhoi Su-30 MKI fighter variant, and the United Arab Emirates (UAE)'s *Pantsyr* air-defence system) being tailored for export customers rather than the Russian armed forces.

Export customer oriented research and production is a positive development for the OPK. It has promoted the longevity of some production lines (such as the Sukhoi Su-30) to afford Russia use of them when its defence budget is substantial enough. In the case of the *Pantsyr* air-defence system, the research was funded largely by the UAE and the finished product will be available for Russian procurement if required.[17] When considering the fact that the Russian State Defence Order (SDO) was expected to surpass the OPK's export earnings for 2006,[18] these foreign funded R&D and production lines will be invaluable for the future re-equipping of the Russian armed forces.

---

16   Anderson, 'CAST indicates Russia's leading 2006 military materiel exporters'.
17   'Pantsyr', in *Jane's Ground Based Air Defence,* Jane's Information Group, Coulsdon, Surrey, 2006.
18   James Murphy, 'Russia to Increase Defence Spending Following Challenging Period for Defence Industry', in *Jane's Defence Industry,* vol. 22, no. 10, 1 October 2005.

Annual arms transfer earnings will probably not increase much past the US$8 billion in 2008; however future export earnings will be augmented by the domestic order book. With respect to future domestic production, the SDO is the mechanism within the Russian defence budget that provides for the equipping and modernisation of military units, as well as the R&D funding for the military each financial year. 2006 was probably the first year that money from the SDO, including major equipment replacement and refurbishment, outstripped exports. According to Vladimir Putin, the 2005 fiscal year was in fact the year that heralded this important milestone for the OPK: 'In 2005 we passed a kind of psychological barrier and now Russia is spending more money on weapons than it is earning from military exports.'[19]

Putin's statement is a slight mistruth, because the 2005 SDO that he was referring to—valued at around US$7 billion—covered Russian R&D funding as well as procurement for the armed forces. Regardless, it was a psychological barrier nonetheless, and will likely be interpreted as a sign of commitment to the OPK as a whole.

Sergei Ivanov announced in May 2006 that the 2006 SDO would equal US$9 billion, with most of the funding going towards military unit modernisation rather than R&D. Furthermore, the 2007 SDO increased to US$11.5 billion, with this trend of 20 per cent annual increases projected to continue out to 2015.[20] These figures indicate that procurement and R&D funding has surged from less than 20 per cent of the total defence budget in 2002 to 44 per cent in 2007.[21] This has not gone unnoticed by other industry analysts who are forecasting a considerably more optimistic future for Russia's OPK.

Thus the Russian defence industry could go from strength to strength given the right economic conditions, industry consolidation, anti-corruption drives and domestic demand. The OPK is currently stable. It may not yet be thriving, but it is showing encouraging signs. The pace and extent of developments within the OPK will be affected by the success of current reforms, and the attention focused on the OPK by Dmitry Medvedev. However, the foundations laid by the Putin Administration suggest that the current positive direction is soundly based.

These domestic orders will be paid for by the growing revenues that Russia is reaping from not only its arms exports, but also its primary resource exports.

---

19   Vladimir Putin cited in Henry Ivanov, 'Country Briefing: Russia—Austere deterrence', *Jane's Defence Weekly*, 28 April 2006, available at <http://www.janes.com/defence/news/jdw/jdw060428_1_n.shtml>, accessed 28 April 2009.

20   'State defense order to grow 20% in 2007', 6 May 2006, available at <http://en.rian.ru>, accessed 20 July 2006.

21   Irina Isakova, 'The Russian Defense Reform', *China and Eurasia Forum Quarterly*, vol. 5, no. 1, March 2007, pp. 75–82 (76), available at <http://www.silkroadstudies.org/new/docs/CEF/Quarterly/February_2007/Isakova.pdf>, accessed 28 April 2009.

The bulk of Russia's Gross Domestic Product (GDP) comes from primary resources, in particular oil and natural gas exports. At the end of the 1990s, Russia was pumping 9 million barrels a day. It rivalled Saudi Arabia as the world's largest oil producer and, while it kept more at home for its own use than Saudi Arabia, it established itself as the world's second largest oil exporter.[22] It seems oil has replaced military might as the mechanism that places Russia back on the map as a major international player.

However, oil and the military are not mutually exclusive, and indeed appear to be becoming increasingly complementary in Russian foreign policy. The 2006 arms deal with Algeria, valued at US$7.5 billion, will be paid for in part by the setting up of oil and natural gas platforms in the Sahara by Russian companies including Gazprom and Lukoil. The money the Algerians make from this venture will then go towards the payment for the arms, as well as the US$4.7 billion worth of Soviet-era foreign debt owed by Algeria to Moscow.[23] Moreover, according to industry expert Dimitri Vasiliev: 'As petrodollars are being pumped into the Russian budget, the country's leadership believes it can afford to increase defence spending at a high pace.'[24]

Current high oil prices have provided the Russian economy with a strong platform for growth, contributing to an annual GDP growth of 6–7 per cent over the last three years.[25] These positive financial results have enabled the government to steadily increase the country's national defence budget and will continue to do so for as long as the price of oil and gas remains high. This situation appears likely, with an International Energy Agency report predicting that fossil fuels will remain the dominant energy source up to 2030. The report predicted that oil would still be the largest individual fuel source by the end of the projected period, although natural gas will witness the highest growth in demand. Furthermore, it indicates that if current government policies around the world do not change, global primary energy demand will grow by 1.6 per cent per year from 2003 to 2030—an overall increase of more than half.[26] These kinds of statistics imply that the resource-rich Russian economy will remain robust until at least 2030 and, pending government policy, this should equate to robust defence budgets over the same period. These strong economic predictions suggest further defence spending increases—a positive development for the OPK.

22   Peter Baker and Susan Glasser, *Kremlin Rising: Vladimir Putin's Russia and the End of Revolution,* Scribner, New York, 2005, p. 278.
23   'Algeria signs $5 billion arms-for-energy deal with Russia', *Military Procurement International,* vol. 16, no. 6, 15 April 2006, p. 1.
24   Dimitri Vasiliev, 'More money for the 1m strong military?' 21 December 2005, available at <http://www.mosnews.com>, accessed 5 February 2006.
25   'Country Briefings: Russia—Economic Data', *Economist,* 17 October 2006, available at <http://www.economist.com>, accessed 7 May 2008.
26   'Energy Projections', The International Energy Agency, available at <www.iea.org>, accessed 28 April 2009.

The outlook for the Russian economy was not always this rosy. Overall economic developments within Russia and the former Soviet Union have traditionally been highly unstable. Nikita Khrushchev tried unsuccessfully to make Joseph Stalin's highly centralised and cult-oriented economic system work effectively without Stalin. Mikhail Gorbachev sought to reform the Soviet socialist economy, to make it more humane and more responsive to the popular will, by introducing certain elements of democracy and of a market economy.[27] His efforts failed. Boris Yeltsin led a revolution that destroyed the keystones of the Soviet planned economy and attempted to quickly replace it with the most liberal of market institutions. The revolution was a double-edged sword: the planned economy was totally destroyed, but this had disastrous consequences for the population at large.[28]

This chequered past makes the turnaround within the Russian economy since 1998 all the more impressive. The performance of the Russian economy on Putin's watch has been the best since 1992, when radical reforms were introduced by Yeltsin and Yegor Gaidar. Helping Putin has been the fact that oil prices rose sharply between 1999 and 2007, giving him the funds that Yeltsin never had at his disposal to pay for defence and higher living standards. Putin also began to take control of the economy by striking at the oligarchs—tycoons who benefited from the status quo and therefore opposed economic reform. Putin targeted individuals who controlled the media, banking and oil industries, and renationalised many of their assets.

Meanwhile, Russian GDP grew by more than 10 per cent in 2000. Inflation at 21 per cent was tolerable, and official reserves of gold and hard currency increased from about US$13 billion to US$28 billion. The recovery from the financial crisis of 1998 was due largely to the increase in the price of oil exports and the favourable effect of the 1998 devaluation of the ruble on domestic industry. The recovery continued in 2001 and 2002 (but at the lesser rates of 5.1 per cent and 4.7 per cent respectively), while 2003 and 2004 saw growth of 7.3 per cent and 7.1 per cent.[29] Former Prime Minister Mikhail Fradkov's very conservative predictions out to 2009 suggest growth of around 5.7 per cent and project inflation to drop below 10 per cent.[30]

Although GDP growth remains below inflation, this is counteracted by the 2005 budget surplus of 7.5 per cent of GDP: budget surplus plus GDP growth is equal to approximately 13 per cent of GDP, outstripping inflation. Add to this the impressive US$120 billion trade surplus, US$245 billion worth of international reserves, and a US$70 billion Stabilisation Fund[31] to safeguard against a drop in

---

27   Dale R. Herspring, *Putin's Russia: Past Imperfect, Future Uncertain*, Rowman and Littlefield, Lanham, MD, 2005, p. 137.

28   Herspring, *Putin's Russia: Past Imperfect, Future Uncertain*, p. 137.

29   'Country Briefings: Russia—Economic Data', *Economist*, available at <http://www.economist.com>, accessed 7 May 2008; and 'Russia—Defence Economics', in *The Military Balance 2006*, Oxford University Press, Oxford, for the International Institute for Strategic Studies, London, 2006, p. 150.

30   Mikhail Fradkov in, 'Russia's GDP to Grow by Annual 5.7% in 2007–2009', 29 May 2006, available at <http://www.mosnews.com>, accessed 12 October 2006.

31   Andrew Rozanov, 'Russia and the G7: Time to Spend', *The World Today*, vol. 62, no. 7, July 2006, available at <http://www.chathamhouse.org.uk/publications/twt/archive/view/-/id/1403/>, accessed 28 April 2009.

oil prices, and the Russian economy looks to be in good shape. A statement in the *Economist* indicated: 'When Mr. Putin became President, its GDP was the world's 10th biggest and foreign reserves stood at US$8.5 billion. Today, Russia's economy is the world's 8th largest, and the reserves are US$407.5 billion.'[32]

In light of these figures, Putin can view economic developments with some satisfaction, but it must be tempered by the fact that the price of oil is not controlled by Russia and cannot therefore be credited to his Administration.[33] Even so, Putin has led an economic restoration of Russia, quite different to the impact of *perestroika* and *glasnost* in the 1980s.[34] Russia is on a path to protectionism under Putin and now Medvedev, who have re-nationalised the resource and defence sectors over the past four years. The outlook for economic reform and continued economic growth over the next several years is positive and this will directly assist the resurgence of the OPK over the same period.

Russia's Growing Share of the Global Arms Trade and Developments within its Export Market

Russian arms have performed very well on the global market. While in the West some states maintain reservations regarding equipment reliability, successes in Asia, the Middle East and now Latin America are irrefutable. In fact, the quality of much Russian equipment sold abroad is seen as comparable to the products of the United States and European manufacturers.[35]

From 2001–2004, the United States and Russia dominated the arms market in the developing world.[36] As is to be expected, the United States ranked first, but, interestingly, Russia ranked second (over France and the United Kingdom) in each of the aforementioned four years in the value of arms transfer agreements.[37] Moreover, Russia actually managed to increase its sales by approximately 57 per cent from 2000–2004, whilst global arms agreements values fell by 12 per cent over the same period. This is impressive, as it means that Moscow actually increased its arms exports during a period of global downturn. Russia made US$21.7 billion in arms transfer agreements, or 29.1 per cent of the total.[38] Again, these figures point to a dramatic increase in both Russian sales and sales agreements within a relatively flat arms market.

---

32   'Putin's People', *Economist*, 25–31 August 2007, p. 11.

33   Herspring, *Putin's Russia: Past Imperfect, Future Uncertain*, p. 122.

34   Herspring, *Putin's Russia: Past Imperfect, Future Uncertain*, p. 137.

35   'Defence Production and R&D', *Jane's Sentinel Security Assessment: Russia*, Janes Information Group, Coulsdon, Surrey, September 2005.

36   For use in Richard Grimmett's report to Congress, the term 'developing world' includes all countries except the United States, Russia, European nations, Canada, Japan, Australia and New Zealand.

37   Richard F. Grimmett, *Conventional Arms Transfers to Developing Nations, 1997-2004*, Report for Congress, U.S. Congressional Research Service, Library of Congress, 29 August 2005, available at <http://fpc.state.gov/documents/organization/52179.pdf>, accessed 28 April 2009, summary section.

38   Grimmett, *Conventional Arms Transfers to Developing Nations, 1997-2004*, summary section.

Importantly, these increases have been accompanied by an important change in the profile of the customers. The traditional arms clients of the former Soviet Union were more often than not poorer developing countries valued for their ideological tendencies and desire for Soviet weaponry, rather than their financial credentials. Many of these traditional Soviet client states received substantial military aid grants and significant discounts on their arms purchases.

After the breakup of the Soviet Union in December 1991 these practices were greatly curtailed, as newly privatised defence industries began the hunt for finance. Faced with stiff competition from Western suppliers, during the global downturn in the arms market in the 1990s, Russia gradually adapted its selling practices in an effort to regain and sustain an important share of the developing world arms market.[39] Rosoboronexport, the sole state intermediary agency for the Russian arms export market, was largely responsible for this resurgence. The strong post-2000 figures are indicative of the success resulting from this shift in policy. Figure 1.1 outlines total arms agreement values, by country, from 1997 to 2004:

Figure 1.1: Arms sales (agreements) ranked by Supplier, 1997–2004 (in constant 2004 million US Dollars and percentage of world sales)

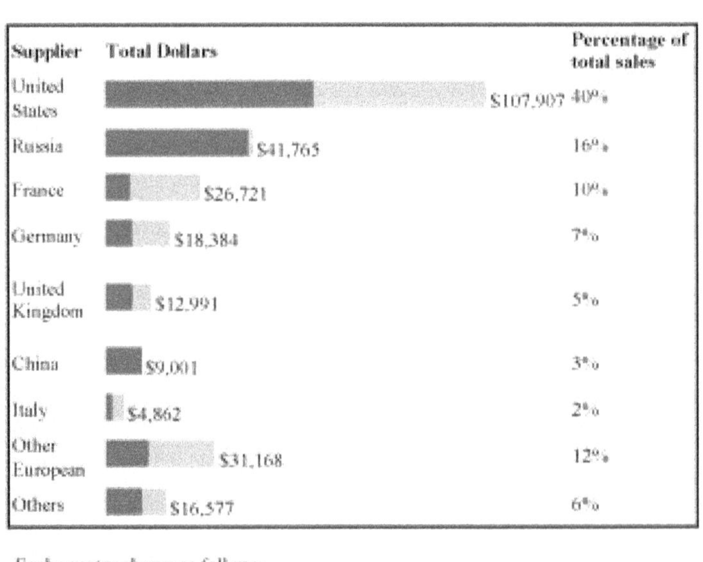

(*Source*: The Grimmett Report, *Conventional Arms Transfers to Developing Nations, 1997-2004*, Report for Congress, U.S. Congressional Research Service, Library of Congress, 29 August 2005, available at <http://fpc.state.gov/documents/organization/52179.pdf>, accessed 28 April 2009)

---

39   Grimmett, *Conventional Arms Transfers to Developing Nations, 1997-2004*, p. 7.

The important lesson from the data in Figure 1.1 is the fact that Russia has near parity with the United States in terms of sales to developing nations. Moreover, over the next five years, the likelihood is that Russia will have overtaken the United States in sales to developing nations, as Russian equipment gains a foothold in a greater number of geographic regions. These developments also come at a time when the United States is losing popularity around the globe, both politically and as an arms supplier.

More recently, the Russian OPK has become aware of the influence of global geo-strategic shifts resulting from the 11 September 2001 terrorist attacks on the United States. These shifts involve the erosion of the previously existing alliance between conservative Islamic regimes and the West, primarily the United States. From an arms sales perspective, one of the first signs of the deterioration of Islamic-American relations began with the 2003 contract for the delivery of 18 Sukhoi Su-30MKM *Flanker* fighters to Malaysia. This contract was estimated as only marginally probable prior to the US invasion of Afghanistan, and was even less probable when considering the problems of serviceability Malaysia had encountered with their other Russian purchase, the MiG-29 *Fulcrum*, and the fact that US F/A-18 *Hornet* fighters were already in the Malaysian inventory.[40] Furthermore, Russia made its first arms sale to Morocco in 2005 (an agreement for *Tunguska* air-defence systems) and has exported to Kuwait, the UAE and Egypt in the last five years, all of which were traditionally recipients of US weaponry.

Russian encroachment into traditionally Western arms markets is not exclusively a result of rising anti-Americanism. It also stems from apprehension within many of these countries (such as Indonesia and India) that the United States is no longer a reliable source of weaponry because of its policy of embargo. Both India and Indonesia have recently had US arms embargoes lifted—India's embargo was imposed after its nuclear tests in 1998, whilst the embargo imposed on Indonesia stemmed from human rights abuses. Interestingly, neither of these nations have purchased sizeable amounts of US weaponry since the embargoes have been lifted, preferring Russian equipment. Indonesia recently indicated its preference for new Russian Sukhoi Su-30 *Flanker* aircraft, rather than spare parts and upgrades for existing US F-16 *Falcon* aircraft. Whilst in some cases less advanced (and indeed less expensive) than US equipment, it is perceived that at least the Russian equipment and its associated spare parts will continue to arrive regardless of any political or human-rights indiscretions.

---

40   Konstantin Makienko, 'Financial Results of Russian Arms Trade With Foreign State in 2004', *Moscow Defense Brief,* 2005, available at <http://mdb.cast.ru/mdb/1-2005/at/financial_results/>, accessed 28 April 2009.

Traditionally seen as the Achilles heel of Russian arms exports, after-sales support has improved markedly in the last few years, and is one area, if tackled successfully, that will help maintain large export figures in the long-term. Concerted efforts have been made by Rosoboronexport and the weapons manufacturers to improve the level of after-sales service for their equipment. Rosoboronexport has opened affiliated servicing agencies in India and China (its primary customers) in an effort to sustain exports and after-sales support—a move mirrored to date in 32 other countries.[41] This turnaround can be attributed to Putin, whose September 2002 decree initiated the process whereby a number of OPK enterprises gained independent access to the spare parts market.

Prior to this, only the arms supplier, Rosoboronexport, provided after-sales support. Contracts for after-sales service are of little interest to state intermediaries such as Rosoboronexport. Unlike arms sales, they require quick and operative work and are not as profitable.[42] However, Rosoboronexport does realise that focusing on after-sales service is a necessary inconvenience, and has made its own efforts to rectify the situation. Therefore, with the relevant enterprises providing after-sales service in an effort to ease the strain on Rosoboronexport in this sector, an altogether more efficient export system is in operation. Alexander Denisov, first deputy director of the Federal Service for Military and Technical Cooperation stated in December 2005: 'Deliveries of spare parts and components for Russian military hardware have grown tenfold in the past two years. In 2003, US$20 million worth of spare parts were delivered, in 2005 we expect US$300 million.'[43]

This expectation of revenue was duly received, and in 2006, US$1.5 billion was made from after-sales servicing and the provision of spare parts, a 500 per cent increase over the previous year.[44] According to Denisov, many pieces of Soviet-era military hardware delivered to various countries are in need of spare parts: a market he believed to be worth approximately US$10 billion.[45] When it is considered that the total volume of the military spare parts market constitutes up to 25 per cent of the cost of the equipment serviced, and up to 40 per cent for aviation equipment, it is easy to see how a figure of US$10 billion is calculated.[46] With after-sales service now firmly in the radar of the Kremlin policy-makers,

---

41   Luca Bonsignore, 'The Future of Rosoboronexport', *NATO's Nations and Partners for Peace*, vol. 49, no. 1, 2004, p. 178.
42   Konstantin Lantratov; Aleksandra Gritskova and Luiza Ignatyeva, 'Military Spare Parts: Abroad *Oriented*', Kommersant, 16 November 2005, available at <http://www.kommersant.com/p625463/r_1/Military_Spare_Parts_Abroad-Oriented/>, accessed 28 April 2009.
43   Alexander Denisov, in James Murphy, 'Russian Defence Exports Decline', *Jane's Defence Weekly*, 7 December 2005.
44   Viktor Litovkin, 'Russian arms exports break records', *RIA Novosti*, 8 March 2007, available at <http://www.spacewar.com/reports/Russian_Arms_Exports_Break_Records_999.html>, accessed 28 April 2009.
45   Murphy, 'Russian Defence Exports Decline', *Jane's Defence Weekly*, 7 December 2005.
46   Lantratov, Gritskova and Ignatyeva, 'Military Spare Parts: Abroad Oriented'.

its weak reputation in this field is slowly but steadily being rectified, and will begin to make itself noticed on the arms export balance-sheet. This factor, in conjunction with successful efforts in market expansion, will all help to retain the larger arms export figures seen since 2000.

Other than after-sales service, another new trend is appearing within Russian arms exports: the growing presence of naval platforms. 2005 was a good year for Russian shipbuilders, with approximately 40 per cent of total arms exports comprising naval equipment. This has enabled several shipyards in Russia to remain open. Shipyards, such as Zelenogorsk, Yantar and Krasnoye Sormovo whose future was far from certain a few years ago, have since completed or are laying down *Gepard* frigates for Vietnam, *Talwar* frigates for India and *Kilo*-class submarines for China respectively. The renaissance in naval exports looks set to continue for the foreseeable future. Boosting revenues from naval equipment, China received the remainder of eight *Kilo*-class submarines and two improved *Sovremennyy* destroyers from a 2003 contract valued at over US$3 billion in late 2006. Short-term sales are also being complemented with much interest in the export versions of the new generation Project 20380 *Steregushchyy* frigates[47] and Project 677 *Lada*-class submarines,[48] both fresh from the Russian design bureaux. Indonesia, Algeria and Venezuela may have already ordered the *Steregushchyy* as part of opaque deals with Moscow—along with Project 636 *Kilo*-class submarines, while India has shown strong interest in the *Amur*-class submarine.

Geographically too, there has been a significant shift in the location of Russia's defence exports. The Far East represents one of the most important geographical areas for Russia as far as arms exports are concerned. Historically second behind the Middle East in terms of arms purchases, Far East Asia moved into first place during the period 2001–2004. Delving further into the figures, Russia actually ranked first in Asian arms deliveries in the 2001–2004 period, with US$4.5 billion more in sales than the United States.[49] Indeed, Richard Grimmett, author of the Congressional Research Service report to Congress entitled *Conventional Arms Transfers to Developing Nations, 1997–2004*, sees this trend continuing for the foreseeable future:

> Until such time as the Indians and the Chinese stop buying as much as they have, and until such time as the Middle Eastern oil barons start making major buys, I don't see this trend changing in the next year or so, it's going to take a while.[50]

---

47   The export variant is known as the Project 20382 Tigr.
48   The export variant is known as the *Amur* class.
49   'Asia overtakes M. East as developing world's arms market', 3 September 2005, *Agence France-Presse,* available at <http://www.inq7.net>, accessed 6 February 2006.
50   Richard Grimmett cited in 'Asia overtakes M. East as developing world's arms market'.

Asia has a significant role to play in helping Moscow revive its defence industries. Such a revitalisation, in turn, would provide an important pillar supporting Russia's rebirth as a major power. China and India have most consistently dominated the list of Russia's defence-related markets in recent years. Trade links have increased and both countries are continuing to produce Russia's most advanced products such as the Sukhoi Su-27 and Su-30 *Flanker* fighters under licence. These links will remain a core market for Russian military products, despite the projected contractions within these markets.[51] The crucial part these two nations play with regard to the success of Russian arms exports will be examined below, and in further detail in chapters 4 and 5.

Arms sales and military technology transfers to China expanded rapidly in the mid-1990s, although many Russian defence officials had strong reservations about sharing advanced technology with such an unpredictable neighbour. From China's perspective, Russia is a source of sophisticated, reasonably priced armaments that are unavailable to them from the West. For Russia, China is another source of hard currency and another market to stimulate OPK resurgence.[52] China has made it clear to Russia that it is interested in developing its armed forces through local weapons development programs based on foreign technologies. Increasing Russian arms sales to China are but one very important sign of a growing alliance between Moscow and Beijing aimed at undermining the US position as the world's sole superpower. After several years of stagnation, Russian arms sales to China were restored in 1991 with 26 Su-27 *Flanker* fighter aircraft worth an estimated US$1 billion.[53] In fact, China was the OPKs primary customer throughout the 1990s.

In particular, China's focus has been on boosting its air and naval force capabilities. Between 1991 and 1996, Russian weapons sales to China were worth an estimated US$1 billion per year. Between 1996 and 2001, the rate of sales doubled to US$2 billion per year.[54] These figures constituted the bulk of total Russian arms exports until 2000–2001, when Indian contracts became more substantial, and Putin, Sergei Ivanov and Rosoboronexport made inroads into other markets as part of an export diversification drive.

China is building a modern air force to operate over the East China and South China Seas. Between 1993 and 1997 it acquired 74 more Su-27 *Flankers*, and the rights to produce 200 more under Russian licence. Su-30MKK multi-role fighters as well as in-flight refuellers and helicopters have also been made. Moreover,

---

51 Robert A. Karniol, 'Russian industry hunts out a future for itself', *Jane's Defence Weekly*, 1 March 2000.
52 Dmitri V. Trenin, 'Russia between America and China', 23 June 2005, available at <http://www.carnegie. ru/en/pubs/media/72788.htm>, accessed 28 April 2009.
53 Trenin 'Russia between America and China'.
54 Ariel Cohen, *The Russia-China Friendship and Cooperation Treaty: A Strategic Shift in Eurasia?*, Backgrounder no. 1459, Heritage Foundation, 18 July 2001, available at <http://www.heritage.org/Research/ RussiaandEurasia/BG1459.cfm>, accessed 28 April 2009.

China has clearly achieved breakthroughs in missile technology by importing systems and prototypes from Russia. It is deploying long-range S-300 (SA-10 *Grumble* and SA-20 *Gargoyle*) air defence systems to protect its short-range ballistic missile bases that are deployed to target Taiwan. It is also developing indigenous surface-to-air missiles (SAMs) such as the HQ-9, which is based on the aforementioned long-ranged and capable S-300 Russian design.[55] As for naval hardware, since 1994 China purchased eight Russian diesel-powered *Kilo*-class submarines and four *Sovremennyy*-class guided missile destroyers. Ariel Cohen, a reputable Sino-Russian defence analyst observes:

> The relationship between China and Russia is symbiotic. China is acquiring capabilities to counter U.S. naval and air power in the Far East and intimidate neighbors like Taiwan. Russia is seeking to become a regional rival to the United States, maintaining its defense industrial base and using money from arms sales to China and others to modernize its own armed forces.[56]

Ever since arms transfers from Russia to China began in 1992, the Chinese market has been the recipient of between one-fifth and one-half of Russian arms exports. No doubt, against the background of the collapse of Russian domestic military procurement in the 1990s, this has helped a number of arms manufacturers to survive. Over the past decade and a half, mutual dependencies have been formed between Russia and China. Essentially, the Russian Government and the defence establishment are satisfied that the Chinese war machine, now and in the foreseeable future, is not focusing on the north, but rather on the east and southeast.[57]

However, the Chinese market will inevitably contract in the coming years as their own indigenous industries improve, so Rosoboronexport and the independent exporters within the OPK have been actively fostering other markets. These include customers in Latin America and Southeast Asia, but these markets have a more limited capacity than that of China. However, in combination with more Middle East contracts, they should ensure that the annual takings for Russian arms remain above US$6 billion.

India and Russia have a tradition of cooperation in armaments that dates back to the 1960s. During the late 1990s, in view of ongoing arms imports by its traditional enemy Pakistan and persistent suspicion of neighbouring China, India needed new equipment from Russia to modernise its armed forces. Among key purchases were Russian technology for armoured vehicles, artillery, and naval systems in addition to aircraft. In early 1996, experts estimated that as much as

---

55   'HQ-9', in *Jane's Ground Based Air Defence,* Jane's Information Group, Coulsdon, Surrey, 2006.

56   Cohen, *The Russia-China Friendship and Cooperation Treaty: A Strategic Shift in Eurasia?.*

57   Trenin, 'Russia between America and China'.

70 per cent of India's armaments had been purchased from Russia. As a result, India still relies heavily on Russia for its arms and Moscow enjoys the rewards of being New Delhi's largest supplier. New Delhi has bought US$33 billion worth of weapons from Moscow since the 1960s and Russian weapons account for nearly three quarters of India's arsenal. For instance, the former Soviet Union and Russia together have built a total of 67 naval vessels for India.[58]

In January 2004, Russia and India signed nearly 20 contracts involving the provision of Russian weapons and technology. One of these contracts, estimated to be worth US$1.5 billion, involved the Russian upgrade of the *Admiral Gorshkov* aircraft carrier and its delivery to India by 2010. India will only pay Russia for the refurbishment of the *Admiral Gorshkov*, which will cost around US$650 million. Additionally, US$730 million will be paid for sixteen MiG-29K *Fulcrum* carrier-borne multi-role fighters, and eight *Kamov* helicopters.[59] Furthermore, Indian reliance upon Russian expertise was highlighted by a development in the licence production of 140 Su-30MKI *Flanker* aircraft by Indian air company Hindustan Aeronautics Limited. The original agreement included full licence production of a number of the aircraft, while the others would be sold by the Irkut company in kit form or fully assembled. However, it became clear in 2006 that completing the order with Indian construction of Russian-made kits, rather than full licence production, would not only save on costs, but also shave three to five years off the final delivery date. This option was duly exercised by the Indians, and has thus given the OPK more work and Irkut an additional US$350 million.[60] Russia has also provided India with 130 T-90S tanks, with 180 more sent in kit form for Indian assembly, and a further 690 to be produced under licence in India up to 2020.[61]

Cooperation between Moscow and Delhi has also seen more than 10 000 Indian military officers educated and trained in the Soviet Union and Russia.[62] In order to maintain the momentum in arms cooperation, Moscow and New Delhi have been steadily advancing their military cooperation into fields such as joint research, development, and co-production. For example, they jointly developed and successfully launched the *BrahMos* cruise missile. India is also collaborating with Russia on joint production of a medium transport aircraft, creatively named MTA. The hope is that this collaboration will prove successful

---

58   Rouben Azizian, 'Russia-India Relations: Stability amidst Strategic Uncertainty', *Special Assessment: Asia's Bilateral Relations,* Asia-Pacific Center for Security Studies, Honolulu, 2004, p. 1-1 to p. 1-8 (1-6), available at <http://www.apcss.org/Publications/SAS/AsiaBilateralRelations/Russia-IndiaRelationsAzizian. pdf>, accessed 28 April 2009.
59   Azizian, 'Russia-India Relations: Stability amidst Strategic Uncertainty', p. 1-6.
60   'Production of Sukhoi Su-30MKI to be hastened, new deadline 2012', 1 September 2006, *India Defence,* available at <http://www.india-defence.com>, accessed 14 January 2007.
61   'Army to acquire nearly 1000 additional T90 tanks by 2020', 4 October 2006, *India Defence,* available at <http://www.india-defence.com/reports-2577>, accessed 28 April 2009.
62   Azizian, 'Russia-India Relations: Stability amidst Strategic Uncertainty', p. 1-6.

enough to warrant a medium fifth-generation fighter joint venture that would complement Russia's own heavy-weight PAK-FA fifth-generation program. More broadly, India is the only country collaborating with Russia on joint production of sophisticated and futuristic weapon systems.[63]

Partly because of the predicted reductions in export contracts with China and to a lesser extent India, concerns that the Russian OPK would struggle to export arms at a level equating to the previous post Soviet record of US$5.78 billion in 2004 have been significantly allayed. As stated previously, the 2008 figure reached US$8 billion. A figure between US$6 billion and US$7 billion seems to be the commonly cited prediction for exports over the next few years. This is in large part thanks to the market diversification drive that has seen renewed successes in Latin America, Southeast Asia, the Middle East and North Africa. It must also be remembered that revenues from arms exports will be augmented with an ever-increasing SDO that reached US$11.5 billion in 2007.[64]

There is currently a Russian arms market diversification triangle that covers three geographic regions: Southeast Asia, Latin America, and the Middle East. In 2006 Russia signed multi-billion dollar arms contracts with Venezuela and Algeria, and Indonesia's acceptance of a US$1 billion export credit offer confirmed that Russian diversification efforts into all three geographic regions have been successful. Rosoboronexport, the state-owned arms exporter, has championed this diversification effort and hopes that the sales to Venezuela, Algeria and Indonesia will stimulate further sales within these countries' respective geographic regions. Recent Russian arms contracts with Mexico, Brazil and Morocco indicate that this ploy has been successful and that the Indonesian arms agreement may generate a similar response within Southeast Asia.

In the Middle East, Iran could potentially return to its pre-2000 status as a strong customer, although the current political situation regarding resumption of their nuclear program will play a major role in future arms deliveries. Agreements during the 1990s between Russia and Iran saw deliveries of Mig-29 *Fulcrum* and Su-24 *Fencer* aircraft, T-72 Main Battle Tanks (MBTs), and Project 877 *Kilo*-class submarines.[65] A subsequent Russian agreement with the United States, the 1995 Gore-Chernomyrdin Protocol, saw the suspension of arms deliveries until 2000. In fact, despite small-scale, post-2000 deliveries, a major contract did not occur until December 2005, when a significant US$1 billion contract for air-defence systems renewed the relationship after a long hiatus.

---

63   Azizian, 'Russia-India Relations: Stability amidst Strategic Uncertainty', p. 1-7.
64   Andrey Frolov, 'Russian Defence Procurement in 2007', *Moscow Defense Brief*, 2007, available at <http://mdb.cast.ru/mdb/2-2007/item1/item2>, accessed 28 April 2009.
65   Grimmett, *Conventional Arms Transfers to Developing Nations, 1997–2004*, p. 8.

Russia has strengthened its commercial position in other Middle Eastern countries such as Algeria, Egypt, Libya and Syria, where it sees a significant market not only in sales, but also replacement and refit of the huge Soviet-era stocks still operated by these countries. The recent US$7.5 billion agreement with Algeria included ships, tanks and aircraft, including a 'buy-back' scheme where Algeria returned two Soviet-era aircraft in exchange for one modernised Russian aircraft—a scheme sure to spike the interest of Libya and Syria, whose arsenals are flush with Soviet equipment. Expansion of the Middle East market has been very successful and has enabled sales to Morocco, Kuwait and significant sales to the UAE—all traditional purchasers of Western equipment. Furthermore, Yemen, a traditional Soviet arms recipient, bought no arms from Russia in the 1990s. Since then, however, it has placed and received significant orders from Russia for state-of-the-art MBTs (T-90), Armoured Personnel Carriers (APCs) (BMP-2 upgrade) and aeroplanes (MIG-29SMT).[66]

Arms exports to Latin America immediately after the Cold War were modest, but the market opened up in the second half of the 1990s. The first exports were in the field of cargo aviation, and especially helicopters. Brazil, Colombia, Mexico, Peru and now Venezuela are the countries from this region that have completed the most important business deals with Russia, including a recent Mexican order for Su-27 *Flanker* fighter aircraft.[67] The military relationship between Russia and Venezuela was established quite recently, but it shows good dynamics and looks to have a very good future.[68] An agreement signed by Hugo Chavez and Vladimir Putin in Moscow in 2001 laid the framework for military cooperation and it bore fruit in 2005 with contracts for small arms, transport and attack helicopters being signed. Future deliveries may include submarines and fighter aircraft, as Caracas moves steadily away from the US camp. This would change the balance of power in South America, necessitating future procurement by Venezuela's neighbours—an action sure to stimulate future Russian sales to the region.

Russian flexible finance policies for arms sales, including possible arms for energy deals, and a visibly increasing presence within Southeast Asia's arms shows, have begun to make an impact in this region. Strong export growth in Southeast Asia has occurred through repeat customers such as Vietnam, Malaysia and Myanmar. These customers have been augmented in recent years with newer customers such as Indonesia and Singapore. The most notable arms agreements for Russia include an unconfirmed 'arms for oil' deal with Myanmar in early 2006 and an export credit offer of US$1 billion to Indonesia.

---

66 Grimmett, *Conventional Arms Transfers to Developing Nations, 1997–2004*, p. 8.

67 Antonio Sánchez-Andrés, 'Arms Exports and Restructuring in the Russian Defence Industry', *Europe-Asia Studies*, vol. 56, no. 5, July 2004, pp. 687–706 (691).

68 'Naval Equipment in Total Russian Arms Exports Equals Over 50 Percent', Agentstvo Voyennykh Novostey, Moscow, 23 August 2005, available at <http://www.interfax.com>, accessed 8 February 2006.

The breakdown of the hardware pertaining to the Indonesian deal included two *Kilo*-class submarines and an assortment of helicopters and armoured vehicles. This was formalised in September 2007 during Putin's Jakarta visit.

While most recent Russian arms sales have been to developing countries within Asia, the Middle East and Latin America, some success is evident in Europe. Russia has managed to sell arms to Greece, France and the United Kingdom, and sales have mainly been of air defence systems (the UK purchase was for Man Portable Air Defence Systems (MANPADS) to be utilised in an anti-terrorist training role)[69]. Sales to France are so far confined to the guided *Krasnopol* artillery shell. On the other hand, a number of examples of collaboration between Russia and France/Italy/European Union has been observed with the MiG Advanced Trainer (MiG-AT), Unmanned Aerial Vehicles, and Russian Regional Jet collaboration respectively.

The other intriguing development within the European arms market has been Russian interest in the defence giant EADS (European Aeronautic Defence and Space Company). Although Putin ruled out a hostile takeover of the company, Vneshtorgbank, Russia's state-run foreign trade bank, acquired a 5.02 per cent stake in EADS in September 2006. There is a possibility that the Vneshtorgbank shares of EADS could be transferred to the new Russian Unified Aircraft Corporation (OAK), if Russian industrial participation within EADS is agreed upon.[70] Needless to say, Russian state involvement in EADS will be beneficial for its own defence industry in the longer-term.

Niche Russian Military Products and the Big Sellers

An important element in the resurgence of arms exports has been the particular niche that many Russian systems occupy. Russian weapon systems offer excellent value for money, as they are both competitively priced and technologically advanced. Russian-made fighter aircraft and helicopters are durable, inexpensive to maintain and come with armour-plating, which enables them to sustain damage from small arms and rocket fire.[71] All of these qualities set them apart from the bulk of their Western equivalents.

A contributing factor to the resurgence of Russian arms exports is the unique capabilities some of these arms possess. Although much of the weaponry is

69   Sánchez-Andrés, 'Arms Exports and Restructuring in the Russian Defence Industry', p. 692.

70   James Murphy, 'Putin moves to allay fears over EADS share buy', *Jane's Defence Weekly*, 4 October 2006.

71   'Defence Production and R&D', in *Jane's Sentinel Security Assessment: Russia*, Janes Information Group, Coulsdon, Surrey, September 2005.

criticised for being less advanced than its US or European counterparts, there are some systems that the West can not better or indeed match. Russian missile technologies, specifically surface-to-air and anti-ship varieties, are widely regarded as being in a class of their own. Furthermore, thermobaric munitions and thrust-vector technologies (TVT) for aircraft engines are fields in which many experts regard Russia as master. Thermobaric munitions are essentially a fuel-air explosive that disperses an aerosol cloud of fuel which is ignited by a detonator to produce an explosion.[72] The shockwave produced from such an explosion flattens all objects within close proximity of the explosion, and further out, soft targets such as personnel face such horrors as the rupturing of internal body organs. These munitions were used to devastating effect during the two Chechen conflicts and, because of their relatively low cost and ease of use (some warheads may be fitted as a standard Rocket-Propelled Grenade), they are an appealing export item.

As ingenious as thermobaric munitions, but far more expensive, is the concept of all-aspect TVT. This is a field in which Russia also excels—US experimentation with TVT still only enables vertical movement (as on the F-35 Joint Strike Fighter short takeoff/vertical landing (STOVL) variant). This technology has been fitted on late-model Sukhoi *Flanker* variants, and the MiG-35 *Fulcrum*. TVT enables 'super-manoeuvrability' which aids dog-fighting, anti-missile manoeuvres and safety at low air speeds.[73] Russia hopes that such technologies will increase the longevity of some of their best-selling defence systems.

Below are the most prolific export items that Russia has sold since the end of the Cold War. Certainly, the T-72, T-80 and T-90 MBTs have sold relatively well, as have the new generation of wheeled BTR family APCs, and tracked BMP family APCs. However, these items are exported at levels far lower than their Soviet forebears, whereas those mentioned below have sustained or surpassed their level of export during the Communist era.

Project 877/636 *Kilo*-class submarines

These Soviet-era submarines are still very capable platforms, due to the high potential for upgrade and the fact that, prior to upgrade, they were already one of the quietest submarines in the world. The original design was the 877, while the 636 variant has improved range, firepower, acoustic characteristics and reliability.[74] Both variants have been widely exported, including to Algeria,

---

72   'Fuel/Air Explosive (FAE)', GlobalSecurity.org, available at <http://www.globalsecurity.org/military/systems/munitions/fae.htm>, accessed 28 April 2009.
73   'Russia Aims to Make its MiG-35 Fighter the Pinnacle of 'Fulcrum' Development', *Jane's International Defence Review*, 1 January 2006.
74   'Project 877 Kilo class', GlobalSecurity, available at <http://www.globalsecurity.org/military/world/russia/877.htm>, accessed 28 April 2009.

Iran, Poland and Romania who received the 877 variant. The biggest customers were India, who received ten 877 variants (all of which are now upgraded), and China, who received two 877 and ten 636 variants. These submarines can be or are already armed with the 'Klub-S' missile system, which fires the vaunted Novator 3M-54 *Alfa* (SS-N-27) missile. The major selling-point for the *Kilo* family of submarines is their acoustic characteristics and the impressive weapons fit that can include a mix of anti-ship or anti-submarine missiles and long-range wake-homing torpedoes. Export orders are expected to continue, with interest from repeat customers such as Algeria and China and new customers such as Indonesia, Venezuela and Vietnam.

Sukhoi Su-27/30 *Flanker* Family Fighters

Perhaps the best performing Russian defence export product since 1991, the development of these remarkable aircraft was far from smooth. After the first 12 had been produced, a complete redesign took place and it is a credit to the aircraft and its design that it survived such upheaval in its early years. In fact, the aircraft went on to break 34 world records in terms of performance and quality of weaponry, and was the basis for a whole family of high-performance aircraft.[75] The beauty of the aircraft from an export perspective is the ability to modify the basic design to suit client preferences. Moreover, the aircraft has proved itself through evaluation against US F-15 *Eagles* and in Indian exercises against both Singaporean F-16 *Falcons* and French *Mirage*-2000s. This glittering record, in conjunction with a very competitive sale price, has led to sales in Africa, China, India, Indonesia, Malaysia, Mexico, Venezuela, Vietnam and the former Soviet republics, as well as interest from Thailand.

MiG-29 *Fulcrum* Family Fighters

Like the *Flanker* family, the Mig-29 *Fulcrum* design benefits from ease of major modification and upgrade. This has preserved its longevity and given the aircraft a new lease of life. Widely exported between 1989 and 2000, the Mig-29 has been exported to approximately 20 countries. A lull in sales then ensued, whereby the only exports were of old Russian Air Force stock to poorer African nations. However, shrewd marketing by RSK MiG, and the introduction of a new, very capable derivative that includes the option for current operators to upgrade their existing fleet and/or procure new aircraft, has seen sales rise markedly since 2003. India, Algeria and Yemen have procured large numbers of the new variant, known as the MiG-29SMT, and Venezuela is another potential customer. The SMT variant rectifies low combat-radius and low airframe lifetime

---

75   Ian Anthony (ed.), *Russia and the Arms Trade,* Stockholm International Peace Research Institute, Oxford University Press, Oxford, 1998, p. 143.

issues that were associated with the original design and also provides an air-to-ground capability not available on earlier variants.[76] India is perhaps the biggest potential customer for this fighter, as it already operates a large number of the aircraft. India has also signed a contract for the navalised variant, the Mig-29K, to operate from the *Admiral Gorshkov* aircraft-carrier, also bought from Russia and currently undergoing refit. India's interest lies not in the SMT variant, but rather the MiG-35, designed with Indian export in mind. This variant is the pinnacle of *Fulcrum* development, and is powered by the uniquely Russian all-aspect TVT. It is a front-runner in the widely publicised Indian requirement for 126 medium multi-role combat aircraft. It is estimated that fulfilling the requirement will cost India around US$9 billion and, if MiG is successful, it will preserve the company's viability for many years to come.

Air-Defence Systems

Cold War military doctrine has played a major part in the success of Russian made air defence systems. The former Soviet Union believed in an umbrella ground-based air-defence network that ranged from shoulder-fired SAMs, to the huge long-range and high-altitude systems that began with the SA-1 *Guild* missile complex. US doctrine evolved to combat such defences and, as such, focused on deep-penetration aircraft such as the F-4 *Phantom* II, armed with anti-radiation missiles designed to knock out Soviet air-defence radars. Today, the legacy of such doctrine is clear to see, with US air-defence systems almost exclusively based on the *Patriot* or recently retired *I-Hawk* systems. Russia's ground-based air-defence systems are far more numerous, and continue to evolve. The most current systems are: the short-range SA-19 *Grisom* missile, on which the mobile *Tunguska* and *Pantsyr* systems are based; the medium-range *Tor* system (SA-15 *Gauntlet*); and the pinnacle of SAM development, the 400 km range, anti-missile capable S-400 *Triumf* system.[77] All of these complexes, or derivatives of them, have been or are expected to be widely proliferated and are well respected by Western analysts.

Mil Mi-8/17 Utility Helicopters

Far less exotic than the air-defence systems, but nonetheless just as important from an export perspective, are the Mil Mi-8/17 family of helicopters. Over-engineered, rugged, and combat-proven, these helicopters have been exported to over 70 countries and remain popular due to their almost legendary reliability

---

76 'MiG-29 SMT Fulcrum', GlobalSecurity, available at <http://www.globalsecurity.org/military/world/russia/mig-29smt.htm>, accessed 28 April 2009.
77 'Russia successfully tests new S-400 air defense system', *RIA Novosti,* 13 July 2007, available at <http://en.rian.ru/russia/20070713/68912072.html>, accessed 28 April 2009.

and low-maintenance.[78] The helicopter has seen over 40 years of service and the latest variant, the Mi-17, is still a popular export choice, with Venezuela the latest customer. Indeed, it was widely rumoured that the United States was a keen potential customer during Operation *Enduring Freedom*. The Mi-17 high-altitude variant was designed as a direct result of Soviet helicopter experiences in Afghanistan and the United States begrudgingly conceded that it was the best helicopter for the job within Afghanistan's rugged and mountainous regions.

The Future of the OPK out to 2015 and Beyond

The aforementioned Chinese and, to a lesser extent, Indian markets will inevitably contract in the coming years as their own indigenous industries improve. This has led Rosoboronexport and the independent companies within the OPK to actively foster other markets. These include customers in Latin America and Southeast Asia—markets that have a more limited capacity than those of India and China. However, in combination with more Middle Eastern contracts, they should ensure that the annual takings for Russian arms remain above US$6 billion. The US$20 billion worth of export contracts will guarantee the workload of the country's defence industry over the next five years.

Moreover, domestic orders through the 2006 SDO equated to US$9 billion, of which nearly 70 per cent (US$6 billion) was spent on procurement and maintenance, and 30 per cent for military R&D.[79] This was followed in December 2006 by the signing of a US$189 billion State Armaments Program 2007–2015, which stipulates that 80 per cent (US$149 billion) of the funding will be spent on procurement and maintenance, and the rest on R&D.[80] Even if these optimistic figures are not adhered to, what does come from the government, in conjunction with the growing export order, will see OPK production lines running steady until the end of the program. The short-term viability of the OPK was never really in doubt. It is the longer-term, beyond 2015, that will require buttressing from domestic and external drivers to ensure OPK longevity.

Predicting the success of the OPK past 2015 is more difficult. There are a number of domestic and external drivers that are required to keep the industry bouyant within this timeframe. Domestically, there are six key drivers. The first is to ensure a more concrete linkage to army reforms within the OPK restructure. Attempts have been made to facilitate this, particularly with the introduction

---

78   See entry for 'Mil Mi-8' in Wikipedia, available at <http://en.wikipedia.org/wiki/Mil_Mi-8>, accessed 28 April 2009.
79   *The Military Balance* 2006, p. 151.
80   Isakova, 'The Russian Defense Reform'.

of the Military Industrial Commission in 2006, headed by First Deputy Prime Minister Sergei Ivanov. This role has given Ivanov more control and input into the structure and workings of the OPK. The second is the promotion of more active attempts to battle endemic corruption within the industry. The current policies must be sustained and more focused, as the problems are deep-rooted and enduring. The third driver has been the most successfully implemented to date: the restructuring of the OPK. This has led to greater efficiency and coordination across the industry as a whole. Fourth, Dmitry Medvedev and Ivanov must ensure that Russia itself becomes the number one customer for its defence industry, by modernising and upgrading significant sections of the defence forces. Rather than the piecemeal attempts that have been witnessed to date, wholesale replacement of Soviet-era equipment must occur so as to sustain large production lines within the defence industry.

The remaining two domestic drivers for long-term OPK success are closely linked to the external drivers. These are the continued success and utilisation of the state arms exporter Rosoboronexport and the requirement of the OPK to commission new joint ventures with India. These joint ventures will provide the OPK with valuable R&D funding, which will sustain it in the long-term as it develops new technologies.

The external drivers required for OPK longevity involve sustaining export earnings from arms transfers. This will occur through the continuation of Rosoboronexport's market diversification drive into Latin America, the Middle East and Southeast Asia. Diversification efforts will pay dividends for the OPK as it will counteract the predicted contraction within the more traditional overseas markets. To ensure that these traditional overseas markets do not contract too much, Russia will probably permit greater technology transfer, or even shift its exports to higher-end niche military equipment. These actions will enable Russia to maintain the high exports figures it has worked so hard to achieve over the last three years.

Chapter 2
The Origins and the Nature
of the Russian OPK

The structure of the Russian defence industry can be very confusing to Westerners and even to industry analysts. The industry differs fundamentally from any Western model because of its Soviet, centrally-planned economic heritage. In order to unravel the complexities of the industry, one needs to look into the history of the Soviet-era military-industrial complex (VPK) and examine developments in the industry under the Yeltsin and Putin Administrations. This background creates a necessary platform for an increased understanding of the contemporary Russian defence-industrial complex (OPK).

The Late Soviet-era VPK

The embryo for Soviet economic advancement—including the evolution of the VPK, came in the form of Stalin's First Five-Year Plan beginning in 1928. The first of twelve Five-Year Plans, it spawned spectacular industrial growth, especially in capital investment. More importantly, it laid the foundation for the centralised industrial planning so often associated with the Soviet Union. Heavy industry received much greater investment than light industry throughout the Stalin period, and this set the precedent for the considerable size of the late Soviet-era VPK.[1] In the post Second World War period, and for the next 40 years of its adversarial relationship with the United States, the Soviet Union tried to compete militarily with an economy several times its size. Viewed in an historical light, the militarisation of the Soviet economy perhaps appears to have been inevitable. However, other nations, even though not as frequently involved in conflicts as the Soviet Union, have passed in and out of wars without their economies being so totally and lastingly dominated by the military sector as did the Soviet Union.[2]

Josef Stalin and his successors, influenced by the Soviet Union's victory over Nazi Germany, believed that the Soviet Union's national security depended on a tried and tested strategy. This involved massive conscript armies, numerical superiority, robust hardware, advanced technologies and extensive military-industrial capacities and reserves. These factors would allow it to fight and

---

1   Library of Congress, Federal Research *Division, Country Studies: Soviet* Union, available at <http://lcweb2. loc.gov/frd/cs/sutoc.html>, accessed 28 April 2009.

2   Clifford G. Gaddy, *The Price of the Past: Russia's Struggle with the Legacy of a Militarized Economy,* Brookings Institution Press, Washington, DC, 1996, p. 33.

win prolonged wars against other mass armies and defend against blitzkrieg assaults. This national strategy put the Soviet Union in a position where it was outspending its post-war adversaries in the field of military procurement. It also made Kremlin leaders receptive to the ingratiation of the VPK, which sought to simultaneously advance its institutional interests while serving the country.[3] The General Staff, the Ministry of Defence (MoD) and the VPK never tired of discovering new military vulnerabilities and devising programs to redress them. These programs usually succeeded in an economy where consumers and rivals could not compete for resources in the marketplace.[4]

VPK expert, Vitaly Shlykov, underscores this reality with two insights. First, he points out that the Kremlin was not entirely oblivious of consumer needs. Structural militarisation was pursued through a policy of 'guns and margarine', which provided the population with a no-frills living standard while freeing up all other resources for defence purposes.[5] Second, this militarisation continued unabated as technological progress increased Gross Domestic Product (GDP) because military doctrine required the MoD and VPK to plan not just for the worst case, but for the unimaginable as well. Therefore, it was imbued in Soviet policy that there could never be too much defence. This *modus operandi* began to change with the accession to power of Mikhail Gorbachev, who was concerned with the size of the defence budget, as a proportion of total Soviet GDP. His calculations were simple: whatever the Soviet Union gained by spending so much on its military was being threatened by its inability to make the rest of the economy work, especially in attempting to raise the living standards of its people.[6] This assessment proved tragic for the Soviet Union in its brutal simplicity and accuracy.

The sheer scale of Soviet weapons production and defence spending is remarkable, especially in light of the post-Communist downward revision in Soviet purchasing power parity in 1989, as computed by Aleksei Ponomarenko, then deputy director of Goskomstat. It indicated that US Gross National Product (GNP) was three times higher than that of the Soviet Union at that time. The Kremlin devoted a disproportionate share of the nation's resources to military activities. The best estimates indicate that the VPK employed 16 million people as well as supporting 6 million soldiers and up to 20 million reservists.[7] The most important attribute of the Soviet production system was its structural militarisation. The institutionally embedded demand for weapons was seemingly limitless and supply capacities were continually expanded. As a consequence,

3   Steven Rosefielde, *Russia in the 21st Century*, Cambridge University Press, Cambridge, 2005, p. 52.
4   Rosefielde, *Russia in the 21st Century*, p. 52.
5   Rosefielde, *Russia in the 21st Century*, p. 51.
6   Gaddy, *The Price of the Past*, p. 49.
7   Rosefielde, *Russia in the 21st Century*, p. 51.

the defence share of GDP rose to 25–30 per cent during the post-war period, with the civilian share diminishing reciprocally. As a result, the only economic success the Kremlin ever achieved was mass weapons production.

With the notable exception of Gorbachev, Soviet leaders have always emphasised investment in military production over investment in the civilian economy. This had very positive effects on the production of armaments within the Soviet Union, some of which were widely regarded as the world's best. The downside was the Communist country's inability to produce basic consumer goods of satisfactory quality or in sufficient quantities. The high priority given to military production has traditionally enabled military-industrial enterprises to commandeer the best managers, labour and materials from civilian plants. In the late 1980s, however, Gorbachev transferred some leading defence industry officials to the civilian sector of the economy in an effort to make it as efficient as its military counterpart.

The Soviet-era VPK also experimented with production of civilian goods. It was during the Brezhnev era that the Soviet Government began to turn to its defence plants for the production of civilian necessities. Though conversion to civilian production was not the order of the day, 'conversion' of the defence sector was attempted through the establishment of factories geared towards the development and manufacture of civilian products within a defence framework. These efforts, however, had very limited results (results that Boris Yeltsin would have benefited from examining prior to his OPK conversion drive in the 1990s). Even though the defence industry was well ahead of the civilian sector in terms of its scientific, technological, and professional standards, a technology gap remained within the defence sector between its civilian and its military level of production.[8] Overall, defence factories produced a maximum of 22 per cent of all consumer goods other than food.[9] This production of civilian goods within the VPK, like that of military products, was heavily subsidised by the state.

The numerous ministries and factories that made up the Soviet-era Military-Industrial Complex were coordinated by the Military-Industrial Commission (also known as VPK). Officially, eight ministries fell under the direct control of the VPK, but numerous other so-called 'civilian' ministries also produced military equipment. In fact, nearly all of the industrial sectors within the Soviet economy were involved in the production of goods used by the military.[10] This formed a vast military-industrial complex that dominated the Soviet economy

---

8   Mikhail I. Gerasev and Viktor M. Surikov, 'The Crisis in the Russian Defense Industry: Implications for Arms Exports', *Russia in the World Arms Trade,* Brookings Institution Press, Washington, 1997, p. 11.
9   Gerasev and Surikov, 'The Crisis in the Russian Defense Industry: Implications for Arms Exports', p. 10.
10   Mikhail Agursky, *The Soviet Military Industrial Complex,* The Magnes Press, Jerusalem, 1980, p. 7.

and ultimately led to structural militarisation: 'The Military-Industrial Commission represented the keystone of the entire system, controlling and coordinating all levels of activity.'[11]

Below the ministries were the defence research and design bureaux, and the factories that made up the Soviet Union's VPK. Western analysts placed these entities into three broad categories during the Cold War: research institutions, design organisations, and production facilities. The research institutions were responsible for scientific research that could be applied within the design organisations. Their responsibilities included planning for new products and machines, and designing new processes, installations and machinery. The new weapons and military material projects developed by the research institutions were progressed from concept to prototype, and then handed off to the production enterprises. The production enterprises were responsible for manufacturing the new product, or applying the process developed by the research and design facilities.[12] For example, there was no single company that designed, built and sold the Sukhoi series of aircraft. There was the Sukhoi design bureau that was responsible for developing the designs and prototypes of the Su series aircraft, but these aircraft were subsequently built by a number of factories located in different regions—the most important being the Irkutsk plant (NPK Irkut) and the Komsomolsk-on-Amur aviation plant.

The Soviet Union of the late 1980s had the largest centralised economy in the world. The regime established its economic priorities through central planning—a system under which administrative decisions rather than the market determined resource allocation and prices. The integration of the Communist party, government, and military within the Soviet Union was most evident in the VPK. It was the Military-Industrial Commission that coordinated the activities of the Defence Council and the Defence Industry Department of the Central Committee.[13] The Defence Council, made up of high-ranking military personnel, was the overarching head of the various research and design bureaux, and it made decisions on the development and production of major weapon systems. Meanwhile, the Defence Industry Department of the Central Committee was the overarching head of the production facilities. The State Planning Committee (or Gosplan) had an important role in directing necessary supplies and resources to military industries.

---

11 Thierry Malleret, *Conversion of the Defense Industry in the Former Soviet Union*, Institute for East-West Security Studies, Westview Press, New York, 1992, p. 7.
12 Refer 'Russia/Soviet Military Industry', GlobalSecurity.org, available at <http://www.globalsecurity. org/military/world/russia/industry.htm>, accessed 28 April 2009.
13 Library of Congress, Federal Research Division, *Country Studies: Soviet* Union.

Soviet-era VPK Structure

Figure 2.1: Soviet-era VPK Structure

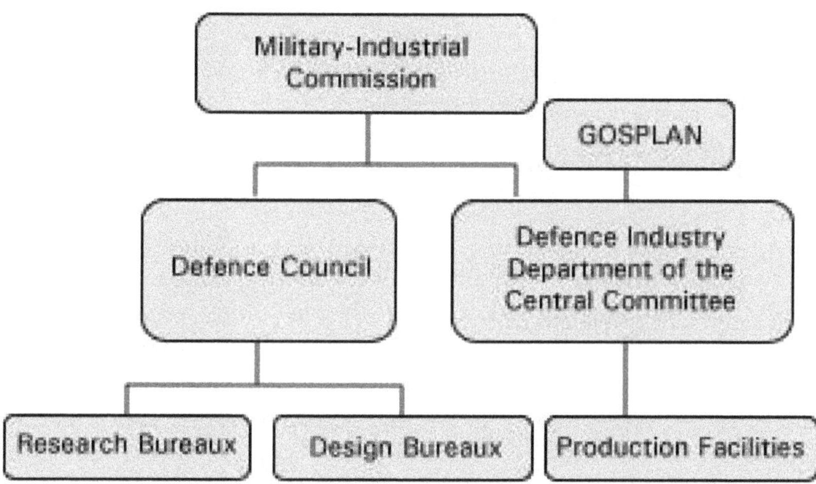

(*Source:* **Cameron Mitchell, based on details noted in Thierry Malleret,** *Conversion of the Defense Industry in the Former Soviet Union,* **Institute for East-West Security Studies, Westview Press, New York, 1992)**

In 1989 the defence industry consisted of a number of industrial ministries subordinate to the Military-Industrial Commission. The names of most of these ministries were not indicative of the types of weapons or military equipment they produced. The Ministry of Medium Machine Building manufactured nuclear warheads. The Ministry of General Machine Building produced ballistic missiles. Other ministries (such as the Ministry of Automotive and Agricultural Machine Building) also produced military equipment and components, but to a lesser extent of their total output.[14] This meant that defence finances were spread amongst a number of ministries, thereby ensuring funds allocated to defence were far higher than was ever publicly admitted by the government.

For example, in 1988 military spending was a single line item in the state budget, totaling 21 billion rubles, or about US$33 billion. Given the size of the military establishment, however, the actual figure was estimated to be at least ten times higher. Western experts have concluded that the 21 billion ruble figure reflects only operations and maintenance costs.[15] Other military spending (including training, military construction, and arms production) may have been concealed within the budgets of all-union ministries and state committees. The amount spent on Soviet weapons R&D was an especially well-guarded state

---

14   Library of Congress, Federal Research Division, *Country Studies: Soviet* Union.

15   Library of Congress, Federal Research Division, *Country Studies: Soviet* Union.

secret. According to US government sources, from the mid-1980s to the collapse of the Soviet Union, between 15 and 17d per cent of annual GNP was annually devoted to military spending.[16] Officially, current Russian Federation defence expenditure (listed as 'National Defence' within the budget) runs at around 2.7 per cent of GNP annually, but, like the Soviet Union, many defence related expenses fall under the responsibility of other ministries. According to the Jane's Information Group, in recent years the aggregation of these extra revenues has boosted defence related expenditure within the Russian Federation to nearly 5 per cent of GDP:[17] it seems old habits are deeply entrenched in the Russian system, and are hard to shake.

Post Soviet Union, the defence-industrial complex went through two distinct phases. The years 1991 through 1997 saw a steep decline, with a focus on privatisation of the defence industry and unsuccessful efforts to restructure defence output into production of civilian goods. From 1998, the emphasis shifted towards increasing and modernising the production of military items. Vladimir Putin revitalised this process in 1999–2000, and also began to renationalise and restructure a large part of the defence industry. These actions have all reinforced the viability of Russia's arms industry in the twenty-first century.

1990–99: The Transition of the VPK to OPK

The term *Oboronnyi-promyshennyi kompleks* (OPK) was introduced in the late 1990s in an effort to distance the Russian Federation defence-industrial complex from its Soviet military-industrial complex predecessor. The term was also assessed to be less aggressive: changing the 'military' to 'defence'. In reality little changed except for the name. It was a facade and the hard work associated with restructure came with the accession of Putin and Sergei Ivanov. This restructure, in conjunction with a greater number of export orders and growing natural energy prices, has finally given the OPK a new identity that goes deeper than just a mere change of title.

The final years of the Soviet regime and the beginning of the 1990s saw increasingly erratic supplies to military producers, a failure of conversion programs from military to civilian production, a further reduction in defence spending, and plummeting exports—all of which caused a decline in defence sector output. Moreover, the military managed to squeeze resources out of the

---

16   Library of Congress, Federal Research Division, *Country Studies: Soviet* Union.

17   'Russia: Defence Spending', in *Jane's Sentinel Security Assessment,* Jane's Information Group, Coulsdon, Surrey, 2006.

state budget, in return for their support during the final year of the Communist regime, and consequently defence spending in 1990 was higher than in any other year during the entire Cold War.[18]

The bubble finally burst in dramatic fashion and, between 1991 and 1995, 2.5 million of the 6.1 million employees left the defence sector. Despite this 41 per cent loss in manpower, in 1996 only 10 per cent of the industry capability was being utilised, rather than the assumed 59 per cent.[19] Between 1992 and 1995, production in the defence sector fell by 60 per cent annually. This was the result of both the sharp deterioration in economic conditions and the lower priority given to the military under Yeltsin. The volume of resources allocated for defence was not enough to finance the reorganisation of defence industries.

Until the early 1990s, the Soviet state was at the centre of the defence industry, providing direction and control to all elements involved in the development of weapon systems. The various elements or enterprises in the VPK did not have Western-style contractual relationships. The plants were all state owned and production complied strictly with the orders of the Party. The state ensured all the enterprises worked together and that no money changed hands between enterprises due to the centralised economy. Furthermore, thanks to a special pricing and taxation system, the defence sector obtained eight times more value for its money than the commercial sector in its procurement of equipment. Economic preferential treatment propelled the VPK to a leading position in the Soviet economy.

Technology advances resulting from the states VPK bias enabled the Soviet Union to successfully compete with the defence industries of the United States and Western Europe throughout the Cold War period.[20] This system broke down with the demise of the Soviet Union. The Russian OPK's adjustment to market economy conditions was difficult because the Soviet-era VPK was always heavily supported and subsidised by state financial resources, inventories, and research/technical personnel.[21] In contrast, the Yeltsin Administration of the early and mid-1990s had neither the ability nor desire to support or subsidise Russia's OPK. Instead, efforts went into restructuring defence output with a focus on conversion of military production into civilian production. Moreover, the new Russian Government tried to transform the system into a market-based one. It proved to be too much change in too short a period for the industry to cope with. Some 75 years of forced conformity had taken its toll on the average

---

18   Paul Rivlin, *The Russian Economy and Arms Exports to the Middle East*, Memorandum no. 79, The Jafee Centre for Strategic Studies, Tel Aviv University, November 2005, p. 16.

19   Robert H. Donaldson, 'Domestic influences on Russian arms sale policy' Presented to the 43rd Annual Meeting of the International Studies Association, New Orleans, 24 March 2002, p. 7, available at <http://www.personal.utulsa.edu/~robert-donaldson/domestic.htm>, accessed 28 April 2009.

20   Gerasev and Surikov, 'The Crisis in the Russian Defense Industry: Implications for Arms Exports', p. 10.

21   Gerasev and Surikov, 'The Crisis in the Russian Defense Industry: Implications for Arms Exports', p. 9.

Russian defence industry worker's sense of capitalism. However, slow transition, longevity of some key Soviet-era technologies and Russian practicality and resourcefulness all helped to ensure OPK survival during this turbulent period.

The serious depression in the defence industry was the result of government neglect and a global downturn in the demand for arms and was a major contributor to the severe domestic economic crisis in Russia throughout the 1990s. Unlike its Soviet predecessor, the Russian Government could no longer arbitrarily set and maintain artificially low prices for military hardware. Nor could it force privately owned parts suppliers and subcontractors to fulfil defence orders against their will.[22] Following the breakup of the Soviet Union at the end of 1991, the Russian Federation inherited a defence sector consisting of 1200 military factories with a workforce of some 4 million. Many more enterprises were partially engaged to fulfil defence orders. Together, they accounted for between 70–80 per cent of the R&D potential and some 80 per cent of the manufacturing capacity of the former Soviet VPK.[23] However, Russia's opportunities to independently develop and produce even model arms and equipment in the early 1990s turned out to be limited because of the need for component supplies from other countries of the Commonwealth of Independent States (CIS). The figures speak for themselves: between 1992 and 1996 munitions production plummeted by 93 per cent, radio engineering products by 93 per cent, and electronic products by 95 per cent.[24]

Soviet industry specialist Dr Michael Checinski noted that maintaining a massive arms capacity within the new Russian Federation could only be transformed into operational reality if three issues were examined: (1) the number and type of weapons to be produced; (2) the time scale for fulfilling the production plans; and (3) how to overcome the bottlenecks in production and distribution that were ever present in Soviet industry.[25] Soviet economic planning gave high priority to addressing these problems and the state-directed pricing policy was one important element in this planning system. As in a market economy, prices were seen as instrumental in achieving efficient distribution of goods and services. However, efficiency was measured only in terms of military security and not against wider social and economic considerations.[26] Soviet methods that were utilised to achieve such efficiency were unacceptable in a democracy (more specifically, were unaffordable in Yeltsin's democracy) and, therefore, the OPK of the Russian Federation suffered accordingly. The OPK today, however,

---

22   Steven E. Miller, and Dmitri V. Trenin (eds), *The Russian Military: Power and Policy*, MIT Press, Cambridge, MA, 2004, p. 160.

23   Gerasev and Surikov, 'The Crisis in the Russian Defense Industry: Implications for Arms Exports', p. 13.

24   Gerasev and Surikov, 'The Crisis in the Russian Defense Industry: Implications for Arms Exports', p. 13.

25   Ian Anthony (ed.), *Russia and the Arms Trade*, SIPRI, Oxford University Press, Oxford, 1998, p. 225, available at <http://books.sipri.org/product_info?c_product_id=162>, accessed 28 April 2009.

26   Anthony (ed.), *Russia and the Arms Trade*, p. 225.

has no requirement to match Soviet-era production and has been able to make considerable progress in adapting to a quasi-market protectionist economy under Putin.

The subsequent difficulties facing the OPK during the immediate aftermath of the collapse of the Soviet Union included the distribution of intellectual property rights, the privatisation of plants and design bureaux, and delayed R&D and production. These difficulties were all attributed to a system of separate research, design and production. Pushing Communist-era structures into a capitalist environment was akin to 'putting round pegs in square holes'. Yeltsin's early 1990s campaign to demilitarise the OPK, the so-called 'conversion', was an attempt to stop it from relying on a dwindling State Defence Order (SDO) and produce consumer products required within a supply and demand environment. Conversion was the main restructuring policy applied in the industry during the first years of the Russian Federation.

Unfortunately, the quality of civil use goods produced by Russian defence plants were questionable and export experience to that point had been exclusively with military equipment and commodities. The scheme unsurprisingly produced poor results—the Sukhoi design bureau was known for its aircraft, not its washing machines or refrigerators. This scheme, combined with a lack of free-market experience and a dearth of government funding, were the main contributors to the gloomy OPK prospects during the 1990s. Even today, civilian use products from Russia are exported at a fraction of the rate of defence related exports, and it is the companies such as RSK MiG and Sukhoi Corporation, or products such as the AK-47 *Kalashnikov,* that are the most widely recognisable in the West. The policy was considered a failure by the mid 1990s, and post 1997, the Ministry of Economy took over the running of the defence industry and changed the direction of reform. From 1997, the aim was still to restructure the defence industry, but by using arms production itself as a fundamental reference point.[27]

Compounding the OPK's problems was the dramatic fall in world oil prices during the early Gorbachev years—a 40 per cent decline between 1985 and 1989, the bulk of the decline occurring in 1986. As a result, the Soviet Union had already suffered substantial losses on actual revenues from arms sales. Oil-producing countries that had been able to pay in dollars for arms could no longer afford to pay in hard currency. In most cases, however, this did not lead to suddenly decreased orders or deliveries; the arms kept flowing, and it took some time before payment was due. But that was not a concern for the producer plants—that was for the government to resolve. As far as the enterprises were concerned, it was

---

27   Antonio Sánchez-Andrés, 'Arms Exports and Restructuring in the Russian Defence Industry', *Europe-Asia Studies,* vol. 56, no. 5, July 2004, p. 687.

business as usual. It took the collapse of the Soviet Union's Eastern European empire in 1989–90 to actually affect the producers, because actual orders dropped then as well. In 1990, there was also a shift in Russia's foreign aid policy. This made it more difficult to justify or mask the subsidising of arms sales even to Soviet non-oil client states.[28] At the end of the Cold War, Russian defence plants lost nearly 80 per cent of government funding.[29] At the same time export earnings were declining due to loss of traditional Soviet bloc markets—especially Eastern Europe. The general decline in the world arms market, and the abundance of cheap, pre-produced Cold War stocks were complicating factors. It was only the slow trickle of hard currency still received from exports to China that kept the industry alive during this transitionary period.

Many analysts believed that the very existence of the Russian defence industry, as well as the nation's military high technology, was in jeopardy. This would have had far-reaching implications for the defence sector and its scientific and technological potential, along with the country's natural resources, which remained the only assets on which to base the ultimate success of economic reform and the retention of Russia's status as an industrially developed nation.[30]

The decline in government contracts for military equipment also had grievous social consequences. Russia lost about one third of its scientific potential over the years of various industry and economic reforms. Scientists involved in computing mathematics, genetics and bio-technologies were usually the first to leave Russia, for the greener pastures of the West. The 'brain drain' became especially active at the end of the 1990s, when specialists started leaving Russia in large groups. According to expert estimates, the total number of people involved in scientific and research works halved from 1990 to 2002.[31] More specifically, the exodus of qualified personnel from defence enterprises has been great. During the first half of 1994, the number of production staff in the defence sector diminished by 15 per cent, up from 12 per cent in 1993.[32] The exodus was mainly attributable to low wages and can still be felt today, although far less so than the mid 1990s levels.

When these exodus statistics are considered, it is amazing that Russia still possesses one of the world's largest defence R&D establishments, both in terms of the number of research centres and employees.[33] The R&D base continues to

---

28   Gaddy, *The Price of the Past*, p. 62.

29   Refer 'Russia/Soviet Military Industry', GlobalSecurity.org, available at <http://www.globalsecurity. org/military/world/russia/industry.htm>, accessed 28 April 2009.

30   Gerasev and Surikov, 'The Crisis in the Russian Defense Industry: Implications for Arms Exports', p. 9.

31   Refer 'With brain drain declining after the period of perestroika, Russia's national intellect is still in danger', *Pravda*, 17 December 2005, available at <http://english.pravda.ru/main/18/88/351/16590_scientists. html>, accessed 28 April 2009.

32   Gerasev and Surikov, 'The Crisis in the Russian Defense Industry: Implications for Arms Exports', p. 15.

33   Miller and Trenin (eds), *The Russian Military: Power and Policy*, p. 160.

survive by maintaining its significant capacity and in many cases prospers—in particular in the cases of developments in aero-engine, submarine, and missile technology. For example, Jane's Information Group has stated that Russia's S-300 family of air-defence systems is highly procurable and also well respected: 'The Russian S-300 surface-to-air anti-missile system is superior to the US-made *Patriot* air-defence system and is also cheaper.'[34]

While the needs of the Soviet armed forces were the dominant factor in planning, at various times the existence of foreign suppliers and foreign markets were probably helpful from both a production perspective (to fill gaps in any given production line) and also in price setting. Goods produced for export were integrated into the overall defence order alongside goods produced for the Soviet armed forces. Furthermore, the chief purpose for exporting these goods was political rather than financial. Soviet foreign policy wielded weapons sales as a means of safeguarding foreign allies' loyalty and enlarging the communist camp. Financial recompense was rarely received if indeed expected—many nations are still paying off Soviet-era debt to Russia to this day. This deficiency in domestic demand, coupled with the lack of market-economy experience in arms exports, were the sources of the subsequent problems faced by the OPK post 1990.

With the dramatic reductions in the volume of state orders, the relative importance of arms exports to the defence industry increased. During the 1990s, the arrears on state payments to the military production facilities came to a figure equivalent to domestic military procurements themselves. In 1996 for example, the accumulated arrears made up nearly half the value of the domestic military procurements accumulated since 1992 and were greater than the orders solicited that year. In 1999, they represented one third of the cumulative internal military orders. This points to the importance of exports for the defence industry. Exports allowed some sense of continuity to be maintained in some parts of the defence industry, which enabled it to avoid the brunt of the economic crisis, as well as the destructive phenomena associated with it.[35] Since 2000, exports have taken on a whole new level of importance, generating a quadrupling in earnings.

1999–2006: The Putin Factor and the OPK

Under the Putin Administration, it became evident that the Kremlin intended to use ownership as its primary control instrument of the OPK. Putin kept

---

34   'Russia: Defence Production and R&D', in *Jane's Sentinel Security Assessment,* Jane's Information Group, Coulsdon, Surrey, 2006.
35   Sánchez-Andrés, 'Arms Exports and Restructuring in the Russian Defence Industry', p. 691.

requisitioning powers in the background and minimised budgetary subsidies at a time when state weapons procurement programs were smaller than those of the Soviet past.

Ilya Klebanov, former Deputy Prime Minister and now Minister for Industry Science and Technology, is Putin's architect for the OPK reform program. Klebanov hopes to reestablish state control over domestic military-industrial activities while creating new entities, such as the Unified Aircraft Corporation, in the anticipation that they will capture a larger share of the global arms market.[36] The melding of design and production makes the new consolidated OPK structures potentially more responsive to domestic and foreign weapons demand and also ensures that designers such as RSK MiG do not rely on regular sales of their products for survival. In essence, more state control over the arms manufacturers will safeguard their survival as they will no longer have to exist solely on the success of their exports.

From 1999, the fundamental principles underpinning defence-industrial reform have consisted of substantially reducing the size of the industry by expelling organisations from the sector and changing to the state controlled structure. As for the policy on arms exports, there has been a tendency to concentrate external orders in a smaller number of companies and, in particular, to assign orders to only a few companies from all of those that could complete them.[37] For example, the military's decision to develop a new tank based on the T-90 at the Ural Coach Works in Nizhny Tagil means that the Transmash factory in Omsk with its T-80 loses out, as the T-80 design was discarded as an option for further development. Furthermore, the MoD approves new designs and finances R&D activities that subsequently bring export revenues to the enterprises and the MoD decides whether or not to permit the sale of various types of armaments abroad. That means any duplication in arms production is avoided. The advantage of this policy revolves around the fact that although there is less variety of production, the country's defensive capacity is not reduced and the government maintains control over the defence industry as a whole.

The aforementioned policies for OPK reform were made official with the advent of the Putin Administration. The Russian Prime Minister in 2001, Mikhail Kasyanov, was the key signatory of government Resolution 713 'On Reforming and Developing the defence-industrial complex in 2002–2006'. He proposed the 'civilianising' of some 1200 enterprises and institutions, stripping them of their military assets, including intellectual property, and transferring this capital to 500 amalgamated entities called 'system-building integrated structures', which the media refers to simply as 'holdings'. The aim is for these holdings to be

---

36   Rosefielde, *Russia in the 21st Century*, p. 94.

37   Sánchez-Andrés, 'Arms Exports and Restructuring in the Russian Defence Industry', p. 699.

51 per cent state owned and to be able to compete with defence giants such as Lockheed Martin Corporation and Europe's EADS. The plant equipment and intellectual property of the more than 1000 enterprises no longer considered a part of the OPK would be transferred into the new holdings.[38]

This rearrangement will increase the military focus of the OPK by divesting it of its civilian activities and also strengthen the defence lobby and augment state ownership. Also, the government is to have a controlling stock of the lead companies (design bureaux) of the system-building integrated structures. This equates to the termination of traditional Soviet separation of design from production and the creation of integrated entities capable of designing, producing, marketing and servicing OPK products.[39] In January 2002, Putin approved this armaments program that called for the 'coordinating, management, and control functions' held by federal entities that manage the OPK to be transferred to so-called system-building integrated structures by 2010.[40] In essence, the plan called for an increase in state ownership throughout the sector by rethinking the privatisations of the 1990s, which officials say lost the government billions of dollars worth of intellectual property. The license production agreement for Sukhoi Su-27 manufacture in China signed in 1994 is a good example.[41]

Up to this point Putin's plan has been largely successful, albeit behind schedule. In 2001, Defence minister Sergei Ivanov was quoted as complaining that: 'About 70 per cent of the military budget is being spent merely to maintain troops and bureaucrats, leaving precious little to maintaining and upgrading equipment.'[42]

However, the following six years have proved that statements such as this have not fallen on deaf ears, and indeed, Ivanov himself has contributed to rectifying the problems aired in his own statement. The SDO has risen every year since, and schedules aside, both Putin and Ivanov are pushing defence industry reform towards ensuring a rise in domestic procurement orders.

As discussed, the main mechanism favoured by Putin and Ivanov for reforming the OPK is the increase in governmental ownership of the complex. This follows the trend set within the energy industry. In the past two years Putin has moved aggressively to reassert state control over Russia's huge oil and gas reserves, which had fallen into private hands in the early 1990s. Putin seems to be 'socialising the guns and privatising the butter' within Russia. There has been little drive to reassert state control over non-primary industry. Primary industry is the main focus, as Mikhail Khordokovsky, the jailed oligarch and

---

38   Miller and Trenin (eds), *The Russian Military: Power and Policy*, p. 167.
39   Rosefielde, *Russia in the 21st Century*, p. 92.
40   Miller and Trenin (eds), *The Russian Military: Power and Policy*, p. 166.
41   Catherine Belton, 'A Call to Arms', 3 December 2001, available at <http://www.businessweek.com/magazine/content/01_49/b3760127.htm>, accessed 28 April 2009.
42   Donaldson, 'Domestic influences on the Russian arms sale policy', p. 7.

former head of Yukos, Russia's largest oil company, found out to his detriment after a questionable and highly publicised trial process. As a result, the Kremlin has already regained more than 30 per cent of the country's oil industry. As the journalist Michael Franchetti wrote in early 2006: 'It's about making the state more powerful. And it's about controlling what Putin thinks are strategically important companies.'[43]

Putin sees the OPK as having strategic importance; hence the move to exercise further state control over the defence industry. Currently 40 per cent of OPK enterprises are state owned, 17 per cent are stock companies with some form of state participation, and 43 per cent are in private hands.[44] These figures were taken with the understanding that a private company had less than 25 per cent state ownership, a state company had 100 per cent state ownership and the remaining 17 per cent of companies had state ownership between 25 and 100 per cent state ownership. Officially, by the end of 2006 (but realistically three or more years thereafter), the government was expected to have a controlling stock in all the head companies of the system-building integrated structures. As a rule, the head company running a holding will be a design bureau. As previously noted, design bureaux were separate from production plants during the Soviet era and were the best known entities of the VPK in the West. Design bureaux such as Tupolev, MiG and Mil were more recognisable than their associated production plants near Moscow, Gorkii and Rostov-on-Don. The new program is intended to put an end to this separation by integrating the design bureaux and production plants into new, vertically-oriented system-building structures. In addition, the state's shares in the remaining enterprises in the OPK holdings will be put into trusts held by the head companies.[45] So in effect, Putin is striving to wrest control of one half of the Russian defence industry from the private sector and orient each of the new entities that are created in such a way that they can research, design and produce the requisite weapon system.

Given the unwillingness of the production plants to share their profits with the state, the government has decided to convert these plants into new holdings (that is, system-building integrated structures). Within the aforementioned government Resolution 713, there would be two stages, both of which are still being implemented with delays from their original deadlines. In the first stage (officially 2002–2004, but now behind schedule), head companies were chosen to develop new weapons and equipment and to establish new integrated structures (holdings) along the lines of existing defence industry branches. The fewer than 500 companies of the OPK that are to remain once the restructure concludes

---

43   Mark Franchetti, 'Putin Flexes Muscles of 'Kremlin Inc'', 1 January 2006, available at <http://www.timesonline.co.uk/tol/news/world/article783971.ece>, accessed 28 April 2009.
44   'Ownership Structure in the Russian Defense Industry', *Moscow Brief,* February 2005, available at <http://mdb.cast.ru/mdb/2-2005/facts/owner/>, accessed 28 April 2008.
45   Miller and Trenin (eds), *The Russian Military: Power and Policy,* p. 167.

will then be divided into these holdings. The plan consists of 40–45 such holdings, with potential options for further consolidation of assets. Integrated holdings have or will shortly be created in aviation, shipping, automobile, radio-electronics, information technology, missile space, ammunition and conventional armaments sectors.[46]

In the second stage (officially 2005–2006, and also behind schedule), the program calls for the creation of new kinds of diversified research and production complexes that will combine enterprises from different branches of industry, produce both military and civilian goods, and be capable of competing in the global market.[47] The composition of every structure, at both the first and the second stages, must be approved by presidential decree. The Ministry of Industry and Energy is responsible for the program overall. The Ministry of Atomic Energy, the Aviation and Space Agency, the Control Systems Agency, the Shipbuilding Agency, and the Ammunition Agency were originally responsible for achieving the program's objectives within their respective branches.[48] However, yet another restructure, this time at the governmental level, now sees the Industry Agency, within the Ministry of Industry and Energy, solely responsible for achieving the program objectives, and this streamlining will greatly assist the overall process of restructure. The overall completion of the reforms within the OPK, factoring in the slippage from the original 2006 goal, is expected in 2010.[49]

Most of the reform policies currently in place or being considered are the concepts of Putin and Ivanov. At the very least, these policies must receive approval from one or both of these figures; thus their importance in the reform of the OPK cannot be underestimated. There have been delays associated with the reform deadlines; hence the discrepancy in the 2002–2006 timeline for the implementation of Resolution 713. However, the overall process is being stubbornly implemented regardless of delay, by Putin and Ivanov and then down the chain of command. The reforms have assisted the OPK to date, but whether the end product ensures that the OPK resembles the phoenix rising from the ashes remains to be seen.

---

46 Irina Isakova, *Russian Defense Reform: Current Trends,* Strategic Studies Institute, US Army War College, Carlisle, PA, November 2006, p. 45, available at <http://www.strategicstudiesinstitute.army.mil/pubs/display.cfm?pubID=740>, accessed 28 April 2009.
47 Miller and Trenin (eds), *The Russian Military: Power and Policy,* p. 171.
48 'Special Report—Russian Defence Industry Rises Again', *Jane's Defence Industry,* 12 January 2005.
49 Isakova, *Russian Defense Reform: Current Trends,* p. 46.

Chapter 3
Domestic Drivers for Russian OPK Success

Essentially, the long-term success of the *Oboronnyi-promyshennyi kompleks* (OPK) success hinges on six key tenets. First, a more concrete linkage of army reforms and the restructure of the OPK is required. Attempts have been made to facilitate this, particularly the introduction of the Military Industrial Commission (MIC) in 2006, which has given Sergei Ivanov more direct control and input into the OPK. Second, active attempts must be made to battle endemic corruption within the industry. Again, attempts have been made in this area too, but it must be sustained and more focused, as the problems are deep-rooted and incessant. Third, and perhaps the most actively attempted to date, is the restructuring of the OPK into a more consolidated sector. The current government push for greater state control over the industry may or may not be beneficial in the longer term; however it is the restructuring itself that is important. Fourth, Vladimir Putin and Ivanov must ensure that Russia itself becomes the foremost customer for its defence industry, by re-equipping significant sections of the Russian defence forces. Rather than the piecemeal attempts that have been witnessed to date, wholesale replacement of Soviet-era equipment must occur so as to sustain large-scale production within the defence industry. The two remaining domestic drivers for long-term OPK success are both closely linked to the external drivers. They include the continued success and utilisation of the state arms exporter Rosoboronexport and the commissioning of new joint ventures with other states. These joint ventures will provide the OPK with valuable research and development (R&D) funding, which will contribute to the viability of the OPK in the long-term as it continues to develop new military technologies.

Linking Armed Forces Reform with OPK Restructure

Since the collapse of the Soviet Union, reform of the armed forces has been one of the most frequently cited objectives of the Russian state; but also one of the most resistant to realisation. The sinking of the submarine K-141 *Kursk* on 12 August 2000 and the elusiveness of victory in the second military campaign in Chechnya only added a few more pixels of resolution to an already clear picture: after nine years under Boris Yeltsin the Russian Army was a shambles. Efforts at armed forces reform had been ill-conceived and inadequately supported financially and politically, and were thus ultimately fruitless.[1] The rise to power of Putin in 1999–2000 signified a change in this area. The military was one of Putin's political tools and strongest partisans during this transitionary period. The new president's initiatives included a National Security Concept and Military Doctrine in 2000; a package of military reform measures in January 2001; and pronouncements of an acceleration of the 'professionalisation' of the army in November 2001. These were followed by a reiteration of the importance of military reform in an address to the Federal Assembly in April 2002, suggesting that the Kremlin was finally resolved to address the problems afflicting the armed forces.[2]

The announcement that the military would focus more on modernisation than reform was a key element to underpinning future OPK economic success, as it meant that re-equipping of units with new military hardware would occur. In October 2003 further policies were tabled in the Duma, this time for the armed forces rather than the OPK, in the form of a Defence White Paper, also known as 'Defence Doctrine', 'Priority Tasks' or 'Ivanov Doctrine'. This comprehensive 74-page document outlined Russia's strategic environment; the tasks of the armed forces; priorities for defence 'modernisation' as opposed to 'reform'; and Russia's multilateral commitments, particularly with the CIS.[3] Putin emphasised the need for civilian control over the armed forces, as well as the need to improve defence management and the structure of the armed forces. As respected Russian defence industry analyst Ruslan Pukhov suggested: 'Ingredient one [for OPK success] is the linking of the reforms within the military and the OPK.'[4]

On 28 March 2001 Putin announced a reshuffle of ministers in Russia's security apparatus. Two senior posts in the MoD went to civilians, with Sergei Ivanov and Lyubov Kudelina assuming the posts of Defence Minister and Deputy Defence Minister respectively. These executive changes had positive implications for financial reform in the military, with Kudelina's budgetary expertise[5] complementing Ivanov's political influence.[6] Moreover, removing Army Generals from these key posts assisted Putin in pushing reforms through the military more quickly and curbed the negative effects of nepotism and corruption within the reform process. Ivanov left the Defence Minister's post,

---

1   Anne C. Aldis and Roger N. McDermott *(eds), Russian Military Reform 1992–*2002, Frank Cass, London, 2003, p. 41.
2   Aldis and McDermott (eds), *Russian Military Reform 1992–2002,* p. 41.
3   Colonel C. Langton (ed.), *The Military Balance 2004–2005,* Oxford University Press, Oxford, 2004, p. 97.
4   Ruslan Pukhov, in an interview conducted at the Centre for Analysis of Strategies and Technologies, Moscow, 6 June 2006.
5   Lyubov Kudelina was a graduate of economics from the Moscow Financial Institute, with over 20 years experience in the Finance Ministry before taking her post within the Ministry of Defence.
6   Aldis and McDermott (eds), *Russian Military Reform 1992–2002,* p. 287.

being replaced in March 2007 by another Putin ally, Anatoliy Serdyukov. The move allowed Ivanov to focus on his ultimately unsuccessful candidature for the Russian Presidency in 2008.

Within the OPK, the Reform and Development of the Defence Industrial Complex Program 2002–2006, signed by then Prime Minister Mikhail Kasyanov in October 2001, reveals that the Kremlin is moving towards a reconsolidation of state authority. The reforms are driven in part by the ageing of the OPK's capital stock; and also underemployment, low pay, and poor enterprise finances.[7] As discussed in chapter 2, the plan envisions the downsizing of the OPK, which currently consists of 1000 enterprises and organisations located in 72 regions, 'officially' employs more than 2 million workers (more realistically 3.5 million), and produces 27 per cent of the nation's machinery and 25 per cent of its machinery exports. The *Voennyi-promyshlennyi kompleks* (VPK) was wholly state-owned at the beginning of the post-Communist epoch. As at 2006, 40 per cent of its holdings remained state owned, 17 per cent were mixed state/private stock companies, and 43 per cent were fully privatised.[8] All of these entities are responsive to the market but retain a collective interest in promoting government patronage, meaning they can be quickly commandeered if state procurement orders revive, which is expected to occur between 2006 and 2015.[9] In the meantime, large contracts for arms from China, India and now Algeria will provide the OPK with the orders it requires to sustain the various production lines of military equipment.

Both Putin and Ivanov realise that if modernisation of the armed forces is achieved, it will greatly assist the longevity of the OPK. The key comparison between Putin's approach and the various reform plans that were put forward during Yeltsin's time is that Yeltin's plans read like a laundry list of items that need to be fixed. Putin's problem-solving approach meant that he preferred to look at specific problems and explore the options to deal with them one at a time.[10] Putin's aim was to set the scene for the large-scale resumption of Russia's domestic procurement program, which in terms of raw finance is now matching arms export revenues. Putin was also trying to scale back the bureaucracies that frustrate both the deployment of new weapons and the operation of conventional arms exports. According to the 2003 White Paper, the proportion of advanced weapons and hardware in the armed forces' entire inventory of military equipment will be raised to 35 per cent by 2010; the armed forces will be totally re-equipped by 2020–2025; and the ratio of the expenditure on weapons

---

7   Steven Rosefielde, *Russia in the 21st Century*, Cambridge University Press, Cambridge, 2005, p. 91.

8   'Ownership Structure in the Russian Defense Industry', February 2005, available at <http://mdb.cast.ru>, accessed 13 June 2006.

9   Rosefielde, *Russia in the 21st Century*, p. 91.

10   Dale R. Herspring, 'Vladimir Putin and Military Reform in Russia', *European Security*, vol. 14, no. 1, March 2005, p. 141.

and hardware to National Defence spending will be raised to 50–60 per cent by 2025.[11] Whether or not Russia can achieve the stipulated deadlines remains to be seen. There will probably be some delays if the reforms and modernisations achieved to date are anything to go by.

In another area of military reform, Putin initially chose to set a rather ambitious target of 'abolishing' conscription by 2010. This policy has since changed to dropping the conscription period to one year by 2008 and the introduction of a program pushing for more contract manning over the same period.[12] Putin's 'one problem at a time' approach is evident within the military reforms, which began with troop reductions, then focused on contract manning, and finally soldiers' pay and conditions. The approach is also evident within the breakdown of funds within the State Defence Order (SDO). SDOs from 2000–2005 saw the majority of the funding going towards R&D, whilst the 2006 SDO looked to be the first of many that devote the bulk of the funding towards procurement of military equipment.

Putin, to a greater extent than his predecessor, understood the dire condition of the armed forces. He cared very deeply about their plight, which is understandable, given his own background in the KGB. The magnitude of the crisis is not lost on him, but the question remains whether he will succeed in achieving real reform, as opposed to 'paper reform'. In appointing Ivanov, a close colleague and a civilian, as Defence Minister, Putin strengthened his own control over the armed forces. He also enhanced the authority of the MoD in forming security policy at the expense of the General Staff.[13] Up to 2004, the General Staff wielded significant power, and had been a thorn in the side of both Ivanov and Putin's reform efforts. On 19 July 2004, Army General Anatoly Kvashnin, who had served as chief of General Staff for seven years, was discharged. He was replaced by First Deputy Chief of the General Staff Yuri Baluyevskiy. Kvashnin, a staunch advocate of a strong ground force, had fallen out with his civilian boss Ivanov over the nature of armed forces reform and the shift to a contract-based recruitment system.[14] Ivanov stressed that the General Staff should be strengthened by clearly redefining the functions and duties of the upper tier of the military. Moreover, he openly criticised the General Staff arguing in 2005 that:

> It spends too much time on superfluous administration and day-to-day management of the troops, to the detriment of its main purpose; situational analysis and development of troop deployment plans.[15]

---

11 'Russia—Tightening State Control', *East Asian Strategic Review 2005*, National Institute for Defense Studies, Tokyo, 2005, p. 183.
12 Aldis and McDermott (eds), *Russian Military Reform 1992–2002*, p. 268.
13 Aldis and McDermott (eds), *Russian Military Reform 1992–2002*, p. 262.
14 'Russia—Tightening State Control', *East Asian Strategic Review 2005*, p. 179.
15 Sergei Ivanov, in Dale R. Herspring, 'Vladimir Putin and Military Reform in Russia', *European Security*, vol. 14, no. 1, March 2005, p. 151.

The removal of the General Staff from a position that wielded considerable influence within policy decisions undoubtedly gave Ivanov more power and flexibility in carrying out further modernisation of the armed forces. In turn, this has given the OPK a greater chance of securing state finances. Ivanov's successor, Anatoliy Serdyukov, was no doubt relieved that he now wielded this power as Defence Minister, because by the 2008 election he needed to have achieved the reduction of conscript service to one year, the introduction of a contract-manning system for non-commissioned officers, and the implementation of a mortgage accumulation scheme of housing provision to servicemen as stipulated in the White Paper. The advantage he now has is that he will no longer have to compete with the Chief of the General Staff in policy decisions, and in addition, he now has a sizeable central staff (unprecedented in either Tsarist or Soviet military organisations) numbering around 9000 personnel with which to achieve these reforms.[16]

A subsequent Presidential decree in August 2004 ensured that the General Staff was relieved of non-military duties including managerial and administrative tasks. The legislation also removed two of the deputies within the General Staff in an effort to de-bloat it. Now there would be only four. In addition the General Staff now assumes the position Ivanov believed appropriate; it has become what the now legendary Chief of the General Staff under Josef Stalin, Boris Shaposhnikov, had called 'the brain of the army'. It no longer attended to operational matters. Essentially, when this bill was adopted by the Duma, Ivanov was placed in charge of all aspects of military affairs.[17] This was clearly aimed at instituting more civilian control over the armed forces and ensuring timelier modernisation programs. For the first time in Soviet and Russian history, the government had established a central control and management apparatus within the MoD and thereby brought all major central staff organisations under the Defence Minister's immediate direction.[18] These moves all appear aimed at strengthening the authority of the Defence Minister over the armed forces as a whole, and follow the general trend of civilianising key positions within the Defence structure.

The stress that Putin has placed on the White Paper as being a modernisation drive, rather than a reform package was purely political. This stipulation had two important electoral benefits for Putin as he chased a second term in office in 2004. First, this sentiment is popular within the military itself, especially at higher levels, because it does not threaten the existing order. Moves for significant reform and reductions in the size of the military appear threatening

---

16　Herspring, 'Vladimir Putin and Military Reform in Russia', *European Security*, vol. 14, no. 1, March 2005, p. 151.

17　Herspring, 'Vladimir Putin and Military Reform in Russia', pp. 150–51.

18　'Russia—Tightening State Control', *East Asian Strategic Review 2005*, p. 180.

to many of Russia's generals. Second, calling it a modernisation drive supports the President's claim that the era of instability and crisis is over, and therefore supports his electoral goals in the population as a whole.[19] The most important implication of the White Paper for military reform is its basic assumption that no more significant changes to the size or structure of the armed forces are to be undertaken; it states: 'Major Armed Forces reductions are not envisioned in the future—their strength has been reduced to the level of defensive sufficiency'.[20]

This implies that the main focus of the MoD is on modernisation—improving training, pay, doctrine, and equipment—rather than on deeper reform. This of course plays straight into the hands of the OPK, as larger and larger SDOs will be forthcoming as the Russian armed forces re-equip themselves with weaponry from Russian defence industries.

In June 2005, all of the proposals within the White Paper were approved at a sitting of the Russian Security Council. The 18-month period between drafting and passing the White Paper was an indication of the potentially massive change the White Paper will have on the Russian armed forces.[21] If the goals within the White Paper are achieved, it will go a long way to assuage the bitter feeling of many members of the Russian military. Russian Army General Vladimir Shamanov summed up the feeling of many Russian Generals when he said:

> Thank God our public has finally begun to discuss the state of the army. Maybe our strategic nuclear forces will protect the country for another decade, but then what? A strong Russia is impossible without a strong army.[22]

Regardless of the terminology, Putin has begun to take the first steps required for genuine Russian military reform. He has pushed the military closer to necessary reforms in the last four years than in any time since the collapse of the Soviet Union in 1991. The reform plan is in place, its funding has increased, some weapons modernisation has begun, and most importantly Putin placed the position of Chief of General Staff under the Defence Minister. Compared with Mikhail Gorbachev, who was not interested in the military, or with Boris Yeltsin, who starved and undermined it, Putin seems to understand its importance and appears committed to dealing with its problems.[23] As Lilia Shevtsova pointed out in her recent book on Putin: 'Whereas Boris Yeltsin was revolutionary, a

---

19   Matthew Bouldin, 'The Ivanov Doctrine and Military Reform: Reasserting Stability in Russia', *Journal of Slavic Military Studies,* vol. 17, no. 4, 2004, p. 627.
20   Bouldin, 'The Ivanov Doctrine and Military Reform: Reasserting Stability in Russia', p. 628.
21   Yuriy Baluyevskiy, 'Igor Baluyevskiy: We do not intend waging war with NATO', *Moscow Rossiyskaya Gazeta,* Moscow, November 2005, p. 2.
22   General Vladimir Shamanov, in 'Iraqi defeat jolts Russian Military', 16 April 2003, available at <www. csmonitor.com>
23   Herspring, 'Vladimir Putin and Military Reform in Russia', p. 137.

man who destroyed the pre-existing Communist system, Vladimir Putin is a bureaucrat, a man who considers his primary task is to bring stability to Russia.'[24]

Putin believes that organisational structures of state ministries such as defence can only be changed by continually coaxing them, and gradually changing their structures, attitudes and personnel. This is why those observers who expected Putin and his hand-picked Defence Minister Ivanov to take the kind of bold decisions necessary to make military reform a reality in a relatively short period of time, were mistaken. Making bold and hasty decisions are not part of Putin's leadership style, and as Russian defence analyst Dale Herspring put it: 'He [Putin] is more the tortoise than the hare—and we all know that in the end it was the tortoise that won the race'.[25]

Perhaps the most important development in the linkage of military reform with OPK restructure occurred in November 2005. Ivanov, while retaining his post as Defence Minister, was appointed Deputy Prime Minister with responsibility for oversight of the arms industry and its relations with the armed forces.[26] Furthermore, in March 2006 Putin approved the formation of the MIC. Ivanov, although retaining his other posts, was appointed chairman. However, the First Deputy Chairman, Vladislav Putilin, exercised day-to-day leadership.

The MIC, much like its Soviet predecessor, is a permanent body exercising oversight of the long-term strategy and planning, and performing operational management of the R&D and procurement projects, but it will also monitor the overall restructuring of the OPK. The body also defines the main parameters for SDOs, including timing, pricing, and personnel policy in the defence enterprises.[27] Its creation has centralised and strengthened the operational management of the OPK, and will no doubt greatly assist the restructuring policies currently in place for the OPK.

Battling Corruption

The problem remains, however, that a large amount of the SDO finance devoted to procurement does not reach the arms manufacturers, and this is why they focus output on the export market. As Konstantin Makienko, of the Centre for Analysis of Strategic Technologies, encapsulated:

---

24   Herspring, 'Vladimir Putin and Military Reform in Russia', pp. 137–38.

25   Herspring, 'Vladimir Putin and Military Reform in Russia', p. 138.

26   Julian Cooper, 'Developments in the Russian arms industry', *SIPRI Yearbook 2006,* Oxford University Press, Oxford, 2006, p. 437.

27   Irina Isakova, *Russian Defense Reform: Current Trends,* Strategic Studies Institute, US Army War College, Carlisle, PA, November 2006, p. 13, available at <http://www.strategicstudiesinstitute.army.mil/pubs/display.cfm?pubID=740>, accessed 28 April 2009.

> Where does the State Defense Order go? You can suppose two reasons only: either all the funds are funneled to the nuclear deterrence forces, to production of Topol and Bulava ballistic missiles, or all budget appropriations disappear in defense ministry lobbies. Only small crumbs make their way to enterprises involved in the State Defense Order.[28]

Steps are being taken to combat the issue of corruption and funds misappropriation within the OPK. According to *Jane's Sentinel Security Assessment*, at the political level, the accountability and transparency of the procurement process has increased as a result of tighter regulatory controls exercised by the Ministry of Industry and Trade. The Cabinet has adopted new procurement regulations, and their implementation is expected to push the overall cost of the defence contract down by 15 per cent. One of these regulations stipulates that all procurement contracts are now to be awarded on a tender basis. Furthermore, bidders will now be allowed to sign contracts only in the first quarter of each calendar year in an effort to tighten fiscal discipline. The cabinet is to introduce a new, 3-year fixed-price type of contract in order to manage procurement costs more efficiently.[29]

Taking over from the old system of individual branch procurement is a new arms procurement agency, the Federal Defence Order Service. It has been set up under the MoD, and its function is to root out corruption and increase efficiency within the military. It has the responsibility of implementing a unified state policy in the areas of development, production, unification, and standardisation of armaments and general-purpose military equipment.[30] The agency, whose management will report directly to Defence Minister Anatoliy Serdyukov, is to put an end to the practice whereby branches of the armed forces themselves sign and oversee defence contracts.

Until recently, all combat arms and numerous directorates within the MoD had the power to commission weapons. This gave the military direct control over substantial cashflows, leaving plenty of room for corruption and funds mismanagement.[31] One such case involved the Vice-Commander-in-Chief of the Russian Air Force, General Dmitri Morozov, who used factories and the budget of the Air Force to enrich himself, his family members and his aides. The Russian news journal *Versiya* obtained documents, from which it emerged that, since 1997, 20 repair workshops for aircraft had been used to generate profits from commercial activities. These profits were laundered through a special Air Force

---

28 Konstantin Makienko, in Konstantin Lantratov, 'Airplanes Will Give in to Submarines. A List of Major Defense Companies Drafted', 9 June 2005, available at <http://www.kommersant.ru>, accessed 18 June 2005.
29 'Procurement', *Jane's Sentinel Security Assessment: Russia,* Jane's Information Group, Coulsdon, Surrey, March 2006.
30 'Procurement', *Jane's Sentinel Security Assessment: Russia,* March 2006.
31 'Procurement', *Jane's Sentinel Security Assessment: Russia,* March 2006.

'charity fund', which was processed and managed by a Moscow bank founded by Morozov and members of his family. The money was used, among other things, to buy luxurious apartments in Moscow for Morozov and his family, the directors of the companies of the repair workshops, the main financial controller of the Air Force, and others who participated in the fraudulent scheme. After this was published in *Versiya* in 2004, Morozov requested retirement.[32] This case is indicative of the culture of corruption that is undermining Putin's efforts to reform the military and OPK. This is the key reason behind the serious efforts that are currently being made to combat corruption.

The appointment of Anatoliy Serdyukov to the post of Defence Minister had two purposes: first, to ensure Ivanov could focus on his Presidential prospects in 2008; and second, to improve the accounting and supervision of MoD spending (Serdyukov was formerly head of the Federal Tax Service). The need to fight corruption, improve purchasing in the defence sector and the ineffectiveness of the MoD's own supervisory institution all played a role in the choice of Ivanov's successor.[33]

Cabinet officials stated that, in the near future, financial controls over the defence budget implementation are to be tightened even further. The MoD is hiring an external auditor to conduct research on market costs of major weapon systems in which the Ministry has an interest. Its procurement and finance agency will introduce a uniform tender format for all armed services and non-MoD security agencies. Weapons will be purchased at fixed prices and the MoD suppliers will be bound by tighter quality control requirements and delivery schedules.[34] This process will be overseen by Ivanov and Putilin within the MIC. It is too soon to assess the probability of success these efforts will have in curbing corruption, but it is noteworthy that this is the first time corruption has been attacked head on. It is certainly a step in the right direction.

Corruption associated with the export of arms to foreign states has also been sharply curtailed, although not eradicated. The November 2000 formation of Rosoboronexport assisted in quelling the rampant corruption within its predecessors, Rosvooruzhenie and Promexport. The government divided its arms export components between these two companies: Rosvooruzhenie managed the complex export contracts requiring the coordination of many OPK enterprises, while Promexport was tasked with managing the spare parts and after-sales support market, as well as any excess Russian military stock.[35] Putin's

---

32   Vadim Saranov, 'Generals of the air force enrich themselves', *Versiya*, Moscow, 25 October 2004.

33   Irina Isakova, 'The Russian Defence Reform', *China and Eurasia Forum Quarterly*, vol. 2, no. 1, March 2007, p. 81.

34   'Procurement', *Jane's Sentinel Security Assessment: Russia*, March 2006.

35   Ian Anthony (ed.), *Russia and the Arms Trade*, Stockholm International Peace Research Institute, Oxford University Press, Oxford, p. 105.

decision to create Rosoboronexport was supported by the many OPK enterprises disenfranchised with Rosvooruzhenie's questionable financial practices. The corruption problem associated with Rosvooruzhenie was compounded with widespread customer dissatisfaction with Promexport's poor after-sales support. Both were telling factors in the creation of Rosoboronexport, which has subsequently diminished, although not completely removed, the corruption problem. Rosoboronexport will be discussed in more detail shortly.

OPK Restructure

The past year [2005] has turned out to be remarkably productive for the restructuring of the defence industry.[36]

Given the scarcity of past domestic financing, the inflows resulting from exports were, and still are to an extent, essential for the OPK's survival. The current approach from the government has been a restructuring policy that uses domestic finances to back those high priority armament programs that cannot receive foreign financing due to international sensitivities (for example, nuclear missiles). Likewise, those organisations that develop high-priority programs that do have the capacity to export may also receive state financing. However, for these last programs and organisations, as well as for those of medium or low-level priority, the financial flows resulting from exports will be of vital importance.[37] Therefore, the companies in which export orders are being concentrated will go on to constitute one of the most important pillars of the future Russian defence industry. Furthermore, their products will be the basis on which domestic military needs are covered and some of the most important Russian arms development programs are established. The policy of arms exports has thus been used as an economic tool to restructure the defence industry and, in the future, it seems that it will play a much more dynamic role in this regard.[38]

Recent defence restructure has focused on industry consolidation, in particular on the aircraft and helicopter sectors. These attempts all stem from the policies tabled in the Reform and Development of the Defence Industrial Complex Program 2002–2006. In 2005, realising the program would expire in one year, the Russian Government ramped up its efforts to integrate the defence industry. According to Makienko, of the Centre for Analysis of Strategic Technologies, the attempt to create a Unified Aircraft Corporation (*Obyedinyonnaya Aviasroitelnaya Korporatsiya* or OAK) was the most important instance of this policy and

---

36 Konstantin Makienko, 'Evolution of Russia's defence industry in 2005', *Moscow Defense Brief*, no. 5, 2006, available at <http://mdb.cast.ru/mdb/1-2006/industrial_policy/item1/>, accessed 28 April 2009.

37 Antonio Sánchez-Andrés, 'Arms Exports and Restructuring in the Russian Defence Industry', *Europe-Asia Studies*, vol. 56, no. 5, July 2004, p. 701.

38 Sánchez-Andrés, 'Arms Exports and Restructuring in the Russian Defence Industry', p. 703.

plans for the integration of the electronics shipbuilding industries are also underway.[39] The close attention paid by political leaders and bureaucrats to the defence industry is unprecedented in the post-Soviet era. The state has taken the first steps towards financing large-scale projects in the aviation industry and integration policy has become less improvised than before, reflecting careful planning.

The OAK is to be created by means of a horizontal integration of the aerospace companies and enterprises within the sector, with the aim of optimising production lines and minimising losses. The OAK intends to bring together all of Russia's main civilian and military companies for building fixed-wing aircraft, together with the main design bureaux. It is envisaged that the state will initially own 75 per cent of the shares of the OAK, but this stake may be later reduced to 51 per cent.[40] However, the procedures involved in the creation of the OAK have been drawn out and the participation of some companies such as RSK MiG could take some time.

Regardless of OAK developments, a kind of informal alliance of former Soviet design bureaux, together with affiliated production facilities, has formed around the axis of MiG-Irkut. At the same time, Sukhoi has preserved and strengthened its status as a strong, autonomous player having the best Russian design bureau among its assets. It is moving forward with the civilian Russian Regional Jet project, is quite self-sufficient and can in principle (barring government intervention) ignore processes of integration. Thus, until such time as the OAK forcibly unites the sector through government intervention, the aviation industry will retain its bipolar structure, with MiG-Irkut and Sukhoi as its two poles.[41] Indeed, with the MiG-Irkut and Sukhoi alliances acting as magnets for the other aerospace designers and manufacturers, a conglomeration of the industry has already occurred.

The consolidation of the helicopter construction industry made considerable headway in 2005, with a leading role played by a Rosoboronexport controlled company, Oboronprom. Acting quietly and effectively, without guidance from a government strategy document, Oboronprom overcame the silent opposition of regional governors and factory managers to consolidate a significant part of the nation's helicopter assets. It has acquired controlling stock in Mil Helicopters, Kazan helicopter plant, Ulan-Ude aviation plant, and Kamov Holdings— effectively the entire Russian helicopter industry except for the company Rostvertol, which it is also keen to take over. All of these firms are expected to be united under a management company called Russian Helicopters, with a

---

39   Makienko, 'Evolution of Russia's defence industry in 2005'.
40   Cooper, 'Developments in the Russian arms industry', *SIPRI Yearbook 2006*, p. 439.
41   Makienko, 'Evolution of Russia's defence industry in 2005'.

possible listing on the Russian stock market.[42] Rosoboronexport's control over Oboronprom is an important factor, as Sergei Chemezov, the Rosoboronexport general director, has since stated that the company now intends to take an ownership stake in all the newly created integrated companies of the arms industry.[43]

Indeed, Rosoboronexport's consolidation of the helicopter industry into Oboronprom was so successful that it has been tasked with overseeing the process of creating all of the holding companies within the OPK.[44] The firm will continue to act as Russia's arms exporter, giving Chemezov an important and influential role in the OPK's development.

The Federal Agency on Industry proposes two state-controlled management companies for the naval construction sector: the Centre for Subsurface Shipbuilding and the Centre for Surface Shipbuilding. The high concentration of private ownership in surface shipbuilding will make the creation of the latter centre an onerous task, involving drawn out negotiations between the state and the private sector. Still, the most important development in the surface shipbuilding industry has been the merger of the two largest (and traditionally two of Russia's most important) shipyards in St. Petersburg: Baltiysky Zavod and Severnaya Verf. This deal finally brought to an end the long-lasting and destructive conflict over who would lead structural reform in the shipbuilding industry. Yet, a tender to construct the second batch of *Talwar* frigates for India was awarded to Yantar shipyard in Kaliningrad (which had struggled to secure contracts prior to this), thereby implying that Yantar could potentially compete at the same level as the St. Petersburg shipyards if further contracts are forthcoming.[45] Regardless, Makienko suggested that the industry overall had made a step in the right direction: 'The defence industry saw during 2005 the birth of some preconditions for a real breakthrough [in sector consolidation].'[46]

Other OPK reforms are afoot, with a new government agency, the Federal Agency for Defence Manufacturing, to be created to supervise further reform. Ilya Klebanov, the former Minister for Industry, Science and Technologies, is expected to head the new body. The government hopes this measure will help it to control the prices of defence products, thereby maintaining a large number of domestic arms deliveries. In 1997 the then President Boris Yeltsin abolished the forerunner (the Defence Industry Ministry) to this agency, which led to the bankruptcy of some defence companies and worsened the state of the

---

42   Makienko, 'Evolution of Russia's defence industry in 2005'.
43   Cooper, 'Developments in the Russian arms industry', *SIPRI Yearbook 2006*, p. 439.
44   Isakova, *Russian Defense Reform: Current Trends*, p. 46.
45   Makienko, 'Evolution of Russia's defence industry in 2005'.
46   Makienko, 'Evolution of Russia's defence industry in 2005'.

Russian defence industry.[47] The two initiatives, and their subsequent outcomes, highlight the differing approaches of the two Russian presidents: Yeltsin's obsession for privatisation and an OPK governed by market forces, a policy which clearly fell short of its objectives; and Putin's more bureaucratic approach of a more centralised and consolidated OPK, which has so far yielded far more promising results.

The Rise of Rosoboronexport

Rosoboronexport is the sole state intermediary agency for the Russian arms export market—known in Russia as military-technical cooperation. There are currently six manufacturing plants within the OPK that are also allowed to export to foreign customers, however, unlike Rosoboronexport, exports from these companies must only consist of products constructed at the plant.[48] The state corporation was formed on 4 November 2000, following a Presidential decree that merged the two previous export companies: Rosvooruzhenie and Promexport.

Currently, Rosoboronexport has the right to deliver a full range of modern weapon systems to foreign countries and to render services on their operation and upkeep. This right sets it apart from the other six OPK enterprises that have the authority to export only the equipment manufactured within their factories.[49] Moreover, Rosoboronexport collaborates with over 700 OPK manufacturing plants, acting on their behalf in foreign trade activities. This enables the corporation to sell the entire range of Russia's export inventory; from *Kalashnikov* assault rifles to submarines. This state approach to arms trading serves two major functions: first, it does not allow too many potential producers to get access to foreign markets because of the possibility that existing rules and procedures for arms exports will be violated; and second, it prevents competition between Russian arms producers for the same market, thereby promoting the longevity of the OPK as a whole. As Pierre Litavrin and Ian Anthony note in their book *Russia and the World Arms Trade*, 'lack of coordination between Russian exporters also resulted in a harmful competition among themselves that weakened the position of Russia on the world market'.[50]

More specifically, unauthorised contracts by Russian arms producers with foreign counterparts in the period 1992–94 had a detrimental effect on the

---

47 'Defense Industry set for Reform', *The Russia Journal*, available at <http://beta.russiajournal.com>, accessed 4 January 2007.

48 Luca Bonsignore, 'The Future of Rosoboronexport', *NATO's Nations and Partners for Peace*, vol. 49, no. 1, 2004, p. 177.

49 Sergei Chemezov in, 'This is Rosoboronexport', *Military Technology*, vol. 28, no. 9, September 2004, p. 39.

50 Pierre Litavrin in, Anthony (ed.), *Russia and the Arms Trade*, p. 107.

military potential of Russia, which Putin does not wish to repeat.[51] For example, the Sukhoi Su-27 *Flanker* contract with China signed during this period gave intellectual property rights away free of charge. The creation of a state-owned military export enterprise largely did away with these problems, as the government managed to exercise control over the private OPK enterprises by forcing them to export arms via Rosoboronexport. Several programs undertaken by Rosoboronexport are of vital importance to the long-term sustainability and profit of the Russian arms export market, including repairs and spare-parts delivery, construction of defence infrastructure within the target market, modernisation of old weapon systems, and a flexible financing policy to ensure the previous programs are affordable.[52]

The after-sales support (repairs and spare parts) market is one in which the Russians have traditionally struggled for credibility. This began to impact on the prosperity of some contracts as the poor repair record deterred a number of potential customers. In response, Rosoboronexport embarked on a public relations campaign aimed at restoring credibility within the service and maintenance sector. This saw the creation of workshops in India, China, Vietnam, Ethiopia, and Mexico, that will provide after-sales support for the weaponry previously sold to these countries. However, the Russian Government has also allowed the various defence enterprises to repair exported defence systems without Rosoboronexport input, to maximise customer satisfaction through the utilisation of the company best placed to repair the weaponry in question. The improvement in this sector was mentioned by Nikolai Novichkov, a Russian defence industry reporter: 'Over the last three years the supplies of spare parts for previously supplied military hardware grew fivefold, and this tendency will persist.'[53]

The market for after-sales support is estimated to be worth US$10 billion, thus both Putin and Ivanov are eager to improve upon the US$1.5 billion earned from it in 2006, be it through Rosoboronexport or the individual defence enterprises.

Rosoboronexport has provided technical assistance for the production of defence infrastructure within many of the countries to which it has exported arms. The construction is often used as a 'sweetener' for potential arms contracts. The Sukhoi Su-27/30 licence-production in both China and India required Russian assistance to organise the production lines and generally prepare the defence industries of both nations for such a large undertaking. It is a policy that few if any Western arms manufacturers follow, which gives Rosoboronexport an edge when it comes to competing for large military hardware tenders.

---

51 Anthony (ed.), *Russia and the Arms Trade*, p. 107.

52 For details about Rosonboronexport, see <http://www.sovereign-publications.com/rosoboronexport.htm>, accessed 28 April 2009.

53 Nikolai Novichkov, 'Russian defence exports surpass targets', *Jane's Defence Industry,* 1 March 2006.

Modernisation of previously exported Russian-made equipment is obviously undertaken in cooperation with the original manufacturers, but it is Rosoboronexport that instigates the agreements. Thanks to this program, Russia is able to cater to poorer nations who could not otherwise afford direct replacement of their old weapon systems. Furthermore, it provides on-site training for operators of the updated systems. Potential financial gains from this modernisation policy are such that some of Moscow's R&D budget allocation has in the past been devoted specifically to the upgrade of 1960s or 1970s vintage systems. Some examples include the successful MiG-29SMT upgrade program (for nations including Yemen, Algeria and India) and the *Pechora*-2M upgrade package for the S-125 (SA-3 *Goa*) air-defence system. It makes perfect business sense for Moscow to focus its efforts on the upgrade of its most widely proliferated Soviet-era weapon systems.

Closely linked to the many equipment modernisation programs is the Russian Government's flexible financing policy. In order to meet customer requirements and requests, Moscow introduced new forms of accounts with foreign clients. Some forms of financing include deliveries of equipment in return for the liquidation of Soviet-era debts (South Korean procurement of tanks, APCs and hovercraft); supplying arms for payment in exchange for the settling of Russian credit (Algeria); barter agreements (utilised by many Southeast Asian nations); and various financial offset programs.[54] This policy has directly boosted Rosoboronexport's sales since the company's inception.

The problem of utilising a state-run company like Rosoboronexport for arms exports is that the process prevents maximum financial return for the OPK enterprise responsible for constructing the arms in question: Rosoboronexport is the 'middle-man'. However, the system's benefits far outweigh its detriments. Rosoboronexport ensures greater government control over exports and enables poorer importers such as Vietnam and Indonesia to procure Russian weaponry through the flexible financing options that would otherwise not be available to them. The figures speak volumes: in 2000 Rosoboronexport accounted for US$3 billion of the total US$3.68 billion of arms exports, and in 2004 accounted for US$5.1 billion of the total US$5.7 billion sales figure.[55] Table 3.1 outlines the magnitude of Russian military exports facilitated through Rosoboronexport, and its predecessor Rosvooruzhenie:

54　Sergei Chemezov in, 'This is Rosoboronexport', *Military Technology*, vol. 28, no. 9, September 2004, p. 39.
55　O. Gertsev, 'Five Years of Rosoboronexport: Trends and Prospects', *Moscow Voyenno-Promyshlennyy*, Moscow, 26 October 2005.

Table 3.1: Russian Arms Exports: 2000–2008
Value of deliveries in billions of USD

Year	2000	2001	2002	2003	2004	2005	2006	2007	2008
Total	3.681	3.705	4.81	5.4	5.78	6.126	6.5	7.3	8.0
Including through Rosoboronexport	2.97	3.32	4.03	5.075	5.12	5.2	5.3	Unk	Unk

(*Source: Moscow Defense Brief*, Centre for Analysis and Strategic Technologies, available at <http://mdb.cast.ru>, accessed 19 January 2009)

Joint Ventures

Despite reticence to allow too much foreign investment within the OPK, the growth in joint ventures over the last 12 years has been impressive. European defence companies such as EADS have been a valuable source of scientific and technical knowledge, whilst Indian companies such as Hindustan Aeronautics Limited have been a valuable source of research funding.

Specifically, the *BrahMos* Anti-Ship Cruise Missile (ASCM), Medium Transport Aircraft (MTA), and potentially, the fifth-generation fighter programs have been conducted in conjunction with India. Russian preference for joint ventures with India stems largely from the fact that India has never needed to directly invest in a Russian company, thereby avoiding potential legal and ownership issues within the OPK.

Joint ventures with European companies include the *Yak*-130 advanced trainer and Mi-38 helicopter. Despite the more complicated legal and ownership issues associated with European investment in the OPK, the *Yak*-130 and Mi-38 have been or are set to be the most successful European joint ventures with Russia's defence manufacturers.

Russia's flagship joint venture to date has been the *BrahMos*. It is a supersonic cruise missile named after the Brahmaputra and Moscow rivers, and is designed and manufactured by Russia's Mashinostroyenia and India's Brahmos Corporation. Its cruising speed is between Mach 2.5–2.8, setting it apart from the subsonic *Harpoon*, its Western counterpart which is about three times slower than *BrahMos*.[56] The missile has been a stunning success, with India's *Rajput* and *Delhi*-class destroyers, and *Talwar* frigates all being fitted with the missile. Air and submarine launched variants as well as land attack variants are also being tested, suggesting that the missile has great utility and good prospects for further orders.

---

56 'BrahMos', at Wikipedia, available at <http://en.wikipedia.org/wiki/Brahmos>, accessed 28 April 2009.

The *BrahMos* experiment proved so successful, that the bulk of the joint ventures either completed, underway or under consideration by the OPK, are with Indian companies or government organisations. India is perceived as a tacit ally by Moscow, and its joint ventures do not include attempts at investment within the OPK. The MTA is due to make its maiden flight in 2012, and is one such joint venture. The MTA would be designed, developed and manufactured jointly and, as its name suggests, would fulfil medium airlift requirements for both the Russian and Indian Air Forces. Furthermore, India has indicated a preference for MiG as the producer of its joint fifth-generation fighter. Indian Defence Minister Pranab Mukherjee publicly acknowledged that India was keen to take part in the development and financing of a MiG fifth-generation fighter with Russia during his November 2005 visit to Moscow.[57] With the success of the *BrahMos* missile, and the high expectations for the MTA and fifth-generation fighter, Indo-Russian joint ventures have paid the most dividends for the OPK to date—plans are now afoot to collaborate on a next generation MBT. The emphasis placed upon them by both the Indian and Russian Defence Ministers suggest that the joint venture concept is one that both countries will continue to adopt in the future.

Although not officially a joint venture, the *Yak*-130 *Mitten* advanced jet trainer, which will enter service with the Russian Air Force in 2006 was assisted by Italy. A contract was signed in 1994 for the development of the *Yak*-130 between the Italian aerospace company Aermacchi, Promexport (one of Rosoboronexport's predecessors), the Yakovlev Experimental Design Bureau and Nizhny Novgorod Sokol Aircraft Plant. Because of its inability to finance the *Yak*-130 project on its own, Russia turned to a NATO member state and its competitor on the arms market for military-technical cooperation. The Yakovlev design bureau received the necessary US$77 million, and the Italians received the plans for the basis of their own M-346 advanced jet trainer.[58] The majority of foreign companies that produce aviation equipment cite the main problem with joint projects in the Russian Federation as the onerous limitations placed on them by Russian legislation. Article 12 of the law 'On State Regulation of the Development of Aviation' of 8 January 1998 limits the share of foreign investors in the authorised capital of Russian aviation enterprises to 25 per cent minus one share and forbids their participation in their management bodies.[59] Furthermore, in March 2006 both the Ministry of Industry and Energy and the Ministry of Economic Development and Trade proposed a draft law limiting access by foreign investors to 'strategic sectors,' which includes 'development, production, overhauling

---

57 'Mukherjee invites RAC MiG to present concept of fifth-gen plane', 2005, available at <http://news.indiainfo.com/2005/11/18/1811-mukherjee-rag-mig-concept.html>, accessed 28 April 2009.

58 Alexandra Gritskova and Konstantin Lantratov, 'Foreign Aircraft Builders Prepare for Soft Landing', 16 May 2006, available at <http://www.kommersant.com/tree.asp?rubric=3&node=25&doc_id=673459>, accessed 28 Apri 2009.

59 Gritskova and Lantratov, 'Foreign Aircraft Builders Prepare for Soft Landing'.

and testing aviation equipment, including dual-use aviation equipment.'[60] What impact this action will have on future foreign investment within Russia's aerospace sector remains to be seen, but it probably will not be very positive. What is certain is that the decision to approve or reject the draft law will have a considerable effect on the future of foreign investment within the OPK.

The Mi-38 project is a good example of the investment issues faced by foreign companies within the Russian defence industry. The helicopter was built by Euromil (a consortium featuring Mil Helicopters and Kazan Helicopters from Russia) and the EADS subsidiary Eurocopter, from Europe. It was conceived as a successor to the Mi-17, sharing many components, but featuring a six-blade main rotor and a redesigned cockpit with new avionics supplied by Eurocopter. After Euromil's creation in 1994, the company was split into 33 per cent shares owned by Mil, Kazan and Eurocopter.[61] After the Russian laws were passed limiting foreign investment in Russian aviation companies to 25 per cent, Eurocopter was forced to withdraw from the project, although this occurred after the maiden flight of the Mi-38 in December 2003. Production began in 2007[62], with state-run Russian oil and gas companies placing orders. This happened without Eurocopter's stake in Euromil, but the legal and ownership issues associated with the program obviously caused unnecessary delays in the helicopter's development.

Despite the problems associated with foreign investment within the OPK, joint ventures are still pushing ahead, especially with India (as it has not yet attempted to directly invest in Russia's defence industry). Russian investment in EADS could also see fewer hurdles arising from that company's association with Russian defence companies. Realistically, however, Russian preference for dealing with India appears to be the most sound plan of action, as it is the one most likely to have the least number of issues in the long term.

Re-equipping the Armed Forces: A Rising State Defence Order

From a purely economic standpoint, arms exports were originally viewed in Russia as the only way to steer the troubled OPK out of its crisis and to save

---

60   Gritskova and Lantratov, 'Foreign Aircraft Builders Prepare for Soft Landing'.
61   Refer 'Euromil Mi-38', *Flug Revue,* available at <http://www.flug-revue.rotor.com/FRtypen/FRMi-38. htm>, accessed 28 April 2009.
62   Refer <http://www.euromil.ru>, accessed 28 April 2009.

national scientific and high-tech industrial potential. Arms exports were also considered to be one of the most important political tools to promote Russia's influence in the world and to boost its international status.[63]

Supporting this argument is the fact that the only OPK enterprises that have managed to thrive are producing arms for China, India, Iran and other foreign buyers. However, should Russia's economic growth and high oil prices continue, it would provide even more resources for the military and security services. In the past 10–12 years, the Russian armed forces have not commissioned large consignments of military hardware and equipment[64]. This is one of the factors behind Defence modernisation being one of Putin's stated priorities. As Russia's ongoing Inter-continental ballistic missile (ICBM) force modernisation program shows, deterrence of both the United States (explicitly) and China (implicitly) remains a prime military security strategy. These nuclear weapons will give the Russian high command the breathing space it needs to compensate for the growing gap in Russian conventional capabilities and military technology.[65] Until the Kremlin is satisfied with its nuclear force, its modernisation will continue to impact on conventional weapons development programs, as considerable amounts of funding continue to be diverted to the nuclear triad. It is no coincidence then that as the export market peaks so too will the level of funding being devoted to the nuclear forces, which Putin stresses are currently being optimised for quality rather than quantity. All signs point to larger slices of the defence budget being directed to conventional weapons procurement.

The traditional reliance on exports to sustain the OPK seems to be in decline. Most industry analysts suggest that a US$5 billion annual export order book should be expected for the foreseeable future. This figure is perhaps slightly conservative, when figures from the previous two years are taken into account— around US$6-7 billion, probably a more likely figure. The SDO for 2007 is stated to be nearly US$11 billion, higher than the level of export earnings, and is set to rise annually.[66] Putin has stated that the armed forces should receive many new types of military hardware in the next few years. There is reportedly a special allocation in the budget stating that 150 per cent more money was to be allocated to the rearmament of the Russian military in 2006.[67] This has meant that the Russian armed forces was to have received 6 ICBMs, 31 T-90 tanks,

---

63   Mikhail I. Gerasev and Viktor M. Surikov, 'The Crisis in the Russian Defense Industry: Implications for Arms Exports', in Andrew J. Pierre and Dmitri V. Trenin (eds.), *Russia in the World Arms Trade*, Carnegie Endowment for International Peace, Washington, DC, 1997, p. 1.

64   Alexander Golts, 'Arming the World: Russia's Lethal Exports', *Moscow News*, 24 February 2005, available at <http://www.mosnews.com>, accessed 28 June 2006.

65   Steven E. Miller and Dimitri V. Trenin (eds.), *The Russian Military: Power and Policy*, MIT Press, Cambridge, MA, 2004, p. 229.

66   Ruslan Pukhov, in Aleksey Nikolskiy, 'The VPK is Losing Clients: Russian Arms Are Not All That Popular in the World', *Vedomosti*, Moscow, 16 June 2005.

67   Olga Belova, (Television Presenter), in 'Segodnaya', *Moscow NTV MIR*, 1000 GMT, 9 November 2005.

125 APCs, 3770 trucks, three submarines, a Tupolev Tu-160 *Blackjack* strategic bomber, several Sukhoi Su-34 (*Flanker* derivatives), and eight Mil Mi-28N *Havoc* attack helicopters in 2006. For all intents and purposes, these purchases are mainly aimed at supporting the weapons manufacturers. Furthermore, the SDO for 2006 covered the upgrade of 139 tanks, 125 artillery pieces, 104 aircraft and 52 helicopters.[68] A 2004 report entitled 'Rearming Russia' stated:

> Given that the Russian military is equipped with weapons manufactured in the 1970s–1980s, we expect to see a massive increase in purchases of new military products in the next decade. But consolidation is the key to survival. We believe that only those enterprises which join the newly formed holdings will have a chance of survival.[69]

In November 2005, Putin announced that the country's economy was robust enough to increase spending on the development of the armed forces. Speaking at a gathering of Russia's top military commanders, he said that, by the end of 2015, the Russian armed forces will have gone through a sustained period of receiving new and refurbished military equipment: 'Only this way will we be able to advance in substantial technical modernisation of the armed forces rather than patching up holes'.[70]

It seems evident from this statement that Putin understands that small-scale equipment delivery and refurbishment will not suffice. The fact that National Defence spending had doubled in nominal terms underscores the priority the Putin Administration attached to rebuilding Russia's armed forces.[71]

These preconditions for armed forces modernisation resulted in the aforementioned State Armaments Program 2007–2015, adopted in December 2006. Unlike its predecessors which focused chiefly on R&D and the creation of military prototypes, this program stipulates a shift towards full-scale production of military equipment.[72] Moreover, it was the first to be formulated by the newly created MIC and 63 per cent of the US$186 billion allocated is devoted to the purchase of new weapon systems.

Since the program was released, there have been some doubts raised regarding the ability of the OPK to satisfy demand. It is already flush with foreign

---

68 Henry Ivanov, 'Russia details weapon procurement plans for 2006', *Jane's Defence Weekly*, November 2005.

69 E. Sakhnova, 'Rearming Russia', United Financial Group (UFG), 2004, available at <http://www.ufgresearch.com>, accessed 12 March 2006.

70 'Putin for Increased Spending on Military Upgrades', *RIA Novosti*, 9 November 2005, available at <http://en.rian.ru>, accessed 13 June 2006.

71 *The Military Balance* 2006, Oxford University Press, Oxford, 2006, p. 151.

72 Ruslan Pukhov and Mikhail Barabanov, 'Challenges to the Reform of Defense R&D in Russia', *Moscow Defense Brief*, Issue 1, 2007, available at <http://mdb.cast.ru/mdb/1-2007/item3/article1/>, accessed 28 April 2009.

contracts for arms over the next five years, and the additional domestic demand will require of the industry an output not seen since the end of the Cold War. For this reason, the program prudently puts off major purchases to 2009–2010, taking export demand into consideration, and therefore allowing for a gradual shift towards full-scale military production.[73] Moreover, the MIC under Ivanov has pushed for government funding to be channeled into the OPK to assist its overall production capacity. The government will devote US$11.5 billion of the US$19 billion required for modernisation and retooling across the OPK, with the rest to come from within the increasingly profitable defence sector. It is the export successes which have enabled the OPK to front up with the remaining funds that will enable it to keep up with demand out to 2015.

Overall, Russian defence industries have proven remarkably adaptable to the post-Soviet transitional economy. Initially there were dire predictions: foreign economists envisioned failed efforts to turn tank factories into tractor plants. Such predictions proved as inaccurate as the false projection of the attempted shift from defence production to civilian production within the OPK.[74] Russia's OPK now possesses the preconditions for improvements in efficiency, including a change in the position of the state with Putin and Dmitry Medvedev rather than Yeltsin at the helm, the stabilisation of the economic situation, and a favourable situation within global markets for primary energy resources. Now the main prerequisite for the sector's further development is the existence of a strategic vision for the future and defining the most promising avenues for financial injections into the high technology complex (that is, R&D).[75]

---

73   Ruslan Pukhov and Mikhail Barabanov, 'Report on Russia's plan for Military Industrial Complex reform', *New Delhi Force*, 1 July 2007.

74   Mark Galeotti and Ian M. Synge, 'Russia's Economy—The Best Case', *Putin's Russia—Scenarios for 2005*, Jane's Information Group, Coulsdon, Surrey 2005, p. 8.

75   'Defense Industry Complex: Punish or Pardon? Does the State need Wings?', *Ekonomicheskiye Strategii*, Moscow, 24 February 2005, p. 1.

Chapter 4
External Drivers for OPK Success:
Arms Transfers to China

In the late 1980s, with the advent of *glasnost* and *perestroika*, some 25 years of Sino-Soviet antagonism ended. Intensive cross-border movements of people and goods were renewed, including the transfer of Russian weaponry for the first time since the ideological divergence that led to the Sino-Soviet split in the 1960s. From 1980 to 1991, China's Gross National Product (GNP) grew at an annual rate of 9.4 per cent, peaking at 13 per cent in the mid 1990s. Since then, GNP growth has held steady between 8 and 10 per cent.[1] GNP growth allowed the Chinese military budget to expand: it doubled between 1990 and 1995, doubled again between 1995 and 2000, and doubled yet again from 2000 to 2005.[2] In March 2006 China announced that its annual defence budget would increase by 14.7 per cent over the previous year. This increase sustained a trend of defence growth rates exceeding overall economic growth that had persisted since the 1990s.[3]

An expanding defence budget has enabled China to carry out major military reforms by refining the numbers of its military and simultaneously improving the quality of technology, weapon systems and training. However, the publicly announced increases in defence spending of around 18 per cent in recent years are difficult to confirm, given the well-known opacity of Chinese figures and statistics, especially with regard to defence.[4] What little public information China releases about defence spending is further clouded by a multitude of funding sources, subsidies, and cutouts at all levels of government, and in multiple ministries.[5] It is likely that this announced spending reveals only the tip of a vast and growing iceberg of military expenditure. The US Defense Intelligence Agency (DIA) believes that the officially published figures substantially underreport actual expenditures: 'DIA estimates that China's total military-related spending will amount to between US$70 billion and UD$105 billion in 2006—two to three times the announced budget.'[6]

---

1   Pavel Felgenhauer in, Andrew J. Pierre and Dmitri V. Trenin *(eds)*, *Russia in the World Arms* Trade, Carnegie Endowment for International Peace, Washington, DC, 1997, p. 89.

2   'Annual Report to Congress: Military Power of the People's Republic of China 2006', Office of the Secretary of Defense, Washington, DC, p. 19, available at <http://www.defenselink.mil/pubs/pdfs/China%20 Report%202006.pdf>, accessed 28 April 2009.

3   'Annual Report to Congress: Military Power of the People's Republic of China 2006', p. 7.

4   Stephen Blank, 'China-Taiwan Arms Race Quickens', 24 February 2004, available at <http://www.atimes. com/atimes/China/FB24Ad01.html>, accessed 28 April 2009.

5   'Annual Report to Congress: Military Power of the People's Republic of China 2006', p. 20.

6   'Annual Report to Congress: Military Power of the People's Republic of China 2006', p. 20.

Since the Tiananmen Square events of 1989, China has been subjected to a Western arms embargo and has had very limited options in obtaining military equipment. Chinese interest in Russian weaponry stems from its limited alternative sources of arms supplies and the commercial benefits associated with dealing with Russia. Commercially, the price of Russian weapons has been lower than other alternative sources. As early as May 1991, the Chinese Central Military Commission drafted a report emphasising that the cost of modernising Chinese military forces with Russian weapons was comparatively cheaper than other sources. It concluded that modernising the People's Liberation Army (PLA)'s military hardware through imports from Russia would help China realise economies of scale within its weapons imports.[7] China's strong desire for Russian defence equipment was compatible with equally strong pressure by Russian arms manufacturers to sell their products to any and all interested parties.[8] China's burgeoning defence budget was a perfect match for Russia's 'preferred supplier' status, selling its weaponry at extremely competitive prices. The Sino-Russian arrangement resulted in a large volume of equipment transfers.

In the early 1990s, the Chinese military continued to lag behind its Western counterparts, both in terms of military doctrine and equipment technology. Chinese authorities deemed the situation critical at the conclusion of the 1990–91 Gulf War, when it became clear that the PLA would be ill-prepared to fight in the air and on the seas against the leading industrialised nations, and some of its closer neighbours.[9] The impact of the Gulf War on Chinese defence strategists was significant, as it demonstrated that large numbers of men and matériel with poor command and control were no match for a smaller, technologically advanced force with state-of-the-art weaponry. The modernisation and refinement of troop numbers in the PLA since the Gulf War was the result of this lesson. The vast majority of the imported military equipment required for this modernisation has come from Russia. According to the Pentagon, China buys about 95 per cent of its new weaponry from Russia, with a focus on aircraft, submarine, destroyer and air-launched, anti-ship-cruise, and surface-to-air missile procurement.[10]

Even though Russia has withheld some of the most advanced technologies that have been sought by China, there is little doubt that Russian assistance in the modernisation of China's armed forces has had a positive impact on their bilateral relationship. In fact, Russian arms sales to China are such a prominent feature of their bilateral relationship that it represents the main link between the two countries—one that motivates and forms the basis of their closer affiliation.

---

7   Ming-Yen Tsai, *From Adversaries to Partners? Chinese and Russian Military Cooperation after the Cold War*, Praeger Publishers, Westport, CT, 2003, p. 120.

8   Pavel Felgenhauer in, Pierre and Trenin (eds), *Russia in the World Arms Trade*, p. 91.

9   'China's Confident Bow; China's increase in defence spending', *Economist*, 10 March 2001, p. 1.

10   'Russia to maintain military cooperation with China—Putin', *RIA Novosti*, 15 June 2006, available at <http://www.rian.ru>, accessed 25 October 2006.

Other than the transfer of weaponry, large numbers of Russian scientists and engineers with long-term contracts also work in Chinese design bureaux and defence plants and Chinese engineers and pilots are partaking in training at Russian facilities and airfields.[11] By 1996, the leaders of the two countries were publicly describing their relationship as a 'strategic partnership' and it became routine for Russia and China to issue joint statements criticising US policy on such issues as NATO expansion, the US-led military intervention in the Balkans and the development of ballistic-missile defences.[12] The Sino-Russian partnership was formalised in December 2000 when the two states drafted the *Treaty on Good Neighbourly Friendship and Cooperation*. The Treaty was officially signed in July 2001.

Although the alliance itself is becoming increasingly significant within the international system, the most important foundational element of the post Cold War Sino-Russian relationship was the arms trade between the two countries.[13] Russian defence industry expert Robert H. Donaldson has suggested that 'Russia sold arms to China in order to buy time and secure the resources needed to ameliorate its most urgent issue, stabilising ... the domestic arms industry'.[14]

The trade of arms from Russia to China was more than just an economic transaction. For China, it accelerated its military modernisation process and provided valuable advancements within its defence industries during a period of arms embargo by the United States and the European Union. For Russia, it provided not only currency, but also the valuable time and resources required to sustain its own defence industry until such time as Russian domestic arms orders became more tenable.

Political and Military Considerations

The transfer of Russian arms to China began somewhat tentatively and fitfully in the early 1990s, but has broadened in scale and scope in subsequent years.[15] It is likely the Russians believe that they can control the flow and scope of these transactions, and that Russian industry will retain control over specific technologies vital to the performance of various higher-end weapon systems. The level of technological sophistication of weapon systems sold to China remains

---

11   Robert H. Donaldson, 'Domestic influences on the Russian arms sale policy', Presented to the 43rd Annual Meeting of the International Studies Association, New Orleans, 24 March 2002, p. 14, available at <http://www.personal.utulsa.edu/~robert-donaldson/domestic.htm>, accessed 28 April 2009.

12   Ted. Galen Carpenter, 'Part 4: Managing the US-China-Russia triangle', 14 November 2002, available at <http://www.atimes.com/atimes/China/DK14Ad01.html>, accessed 28 April 2009.

13   Donaldson, 'Domestic influences on the Russian arms sale policy', p. 15.

14   Donaldson, 'Domestic influences on the Russian arms sale policy', p. 15.

15   Alexander A. Sergounin and Sergey V. Subbotin, *Russian Arms Transfers to East Asia in the 1990s,* SIPRI Research Report No. 15, Oxford University Press, Oxford, 1999, p. 15.

relatively low, considering what the Russian OPK is capable of producing. This policy stems partly from the conservative military-technical strategy of the Chinese leadership. More importantly, it is also a natural consequence of the limits on arms transfers imposed by the Russian military, due to longstanding mistrust and fears of a resurgent China.

For Russia, the major difference in its perception of China and India—its two largest defence customers—is that, traditionally, China has been perceived as a potential security threat to Russia while India has not been viewed as such. Despite the ease of production and delivery of second-tier military systems to China, Russian policy on arms transfer has provoked much grievance from some isolated Chinese quarters. Ming-Yen Tsai, author of *From Adversaries to Partners*, interviewed several Chinese experts, who complained that Russia had not sold China its best weapons.[16] Under these circumstances, China has continued to develop next-generation weapons indigenously. In explaining why China sought to develop the JH-7 (FB-7 *Flounder)* fighter-bomber, the aircraft's general designer, Chen Yi-jian, stressed: 'China is unlikely to buy the latest weapons from abroad. Foreign states usually retain important technologies while exporting arms.'[17]

A supporting example was the delivery of the Su-30MKK multi-role fighter to China. Whilst the Su-30MKK is a capable platform in its own right, the Indian Air Force received the more capable Su-30MKI during the same period. The Indian variant possessed thrust-vectoring engines, canards to assist manoeuvrability, and an improved avionics suite.

The net result is that China receives large deliveries of well-tested armaments with minimal risk of technological failure. Chinese orders are simple and are executed without the major delays and problems with quality control that have plagued Indian orders. By the end of 2003 China had already received about 150 Su-27SK/UBK and Su-30MKK fighters, not including the 100 or so fighters acquired through licenced assembly. By that time India, in comparison, had only received 40 Su-30K/MKI fighters.[18] Russian arms industry specialist Konstantin Makienko commented on arms transfers to China in 2004: 'Chinese contracts concluded after 1999 involve high volume serial production and make relatively few demands for modernization of base models. Such terms are well suited to the Russian military-industrial complex in its present state.'[19]

---

16   Ming-Yen, *From Adversaries to Partners? Chinese and Russian Military Cooperation after the Cold War*, p. 126.
17   Ming-Yen, *From Adversaries to Partners? Chinese and Russian Military Cooperation after the Cold War*, p. 126.
18   Konstantin Makienko, 'The Russian-Chinese Arms Trade: an Attempt at Qualitative Analysis', *Moscow Defense Brief*, 2004, available at <http://mdb.cast.ru>, accessed 22 November 2005.
19   Makienko, 'The Russian-Chinese Arms Trade: an Attempt at Qualitative Analysis'.

However, there are indications that the mutual distrust and wariness is easing somewhat between the two powers. Politically, this is symbolised by the creation in 2001 of the Shanghai Cooperation Organisation (SCO). The SCO consists of Russia, China, Kazakhstan, Uzbekistan, Kyrgyzstan and Tajikistan and, officially, its *raison d'être* is to combat Islamic extremism. However, as various SCO statements and communiques make clear, an important secondary motive has emerged—namely to offset America's increasingly dominant position in Asia.[20]

Militarily, the easing of mutual distrust was highlighted by the combined arms exercise known as *Peace Mission 2005*. In essence, it was a large military exercise comprising Russian and Chinese forces held on China's Shandong Peninsula in August 2005. The code-name *Peace Mission 2005* appeared in the press in June 2005 following a meeting between China's Assistant Chief of Staff, Major-General Chzhan Tsinyein, and Russia's Commander of the Far Eastern Military District, General Yury Yakubov, in the Russian far-eastern city of Khabarovsk.[21] *Peace Mission 2005* was split into three phases: a counter-terrorism exercise, seaborne and airborne troop deployment, and an anti-shipping exercise, utilising both air and naval assets from both countries. Russian forces included strategic bombers, advanced early warning, transport, refueling and fighter aircraft along with modern naval vessels, suggesting the exercise also served as a showcase of Russian equipment to prospective Chinese buyers.[22] Observers from Iran and India were also present, allowing the capability of the equipment on show to also be demonstrated to military officials of these countries. It was the first event of its kind for the Russian and Chinese armed forces and, following the successful conclusion of the second such exercise in August 2007, it looks set to be an ongoing biennial event.

These political and military developments between the two states are clear indications of closer ties, and future arms transfers may well be more advanced in nature than those seen previously. Indeed, immediately following the exercise, China flagged its interest with Rosoboronexport in acquiring 34 Il-76 *Candid* transport aircraft and four Il-78 *Midas* airborne refueller variants.[23] Later in 2005 a contract was subsequently signed for delivery of both aircraft types, which were present at the *Peace Mission 2005* exercise. It was the first time that Russia had agreed to sell airborne refuellers to China.

---

20   Carpenter, 'Part 4: Managing the US–China-Russia triangle'.

21   Mikhail Lukin, 'Peace Mission 2005: A 1970s Template for Sino-Russian 'Peacekeeping'', *Moscow Defense Brief,* 2005, available at <http://mdb.cast.ru/mdb/2-2005/af/peacekeeping/>, accessed 28 April 2009.

22   'Annual Report to Congress: Military Power of the People's Republic of China 2006', p. 2.

23   Marcel de Haas, 'Russian–Chinese military exercises and their wider perspective: Power play in Central Asia', Conflict Studies and Research Centre, Defence Academy of the United Kingdom, Shrivenham, Wiltshire, 2005, p. 1, available at <http://www.clingendael.nl/publications/2005/20051000_cscp_haas.pdf>, accessed 23 April 2009.

State of the Chinese Market

The systems China purchased prior to the Il-76/78 aircraft include the Su-27/30 fighter, advanced air-to-air missiles, S-300 (SA-10/20) and Tor (SA-15) anti-aircraft missile systems, *Sovremennyy* destroyers, and *Kilo*-class submarines with the associated *Klub* (SS-N-27) missile system. These weapons have been described in *Jane's Intelligence Review* by a Chinese source as 'stopgap acquisitions'. It is also telling that, according to Russian sources, China is purchasing more technologies for production from Russia than actual weapon systems.[24] China's aim in doing this has been to develop an indigenous capacity for producing advanced weapons in an effort to reduce its reliance on military imports from foreign states. For example, China has utilised the technologies acquired from Russia to build its own indigenous weapon systems: the new Type 052 air-defence destroyers now under construction, the J-10 fighter aircraft, and the *Yuan*-class submarines. At present, the Chinese continue to rely on critical Russian components for several of its weapon production programs and, in some cases, has purchased the production rights to Russian weapon systems. Russia continues to cooperate with China on technical, design, and material support for numerous weapons and space systems.[25] Thus, it is acquiring, according to most estimates, US$2 billion worth of arms and technologies annually from the Russian defence industry.

Russian industry experts are also talking about selling China even more advanced systems to maintain Chinese demand and remain technologically competitive after China's indigenous defence industry assimilates the technology that is currently being provided by Russia.[26] This would be a departure from the traditional Russian reticence to export its most advanced military capabilities to China and could indicate that the Russian defence industry has even more advanced military technology under development. Conducting exercises such as *Peace Mission 2005* with China is an astute method for providing the Russian General Staff with an insight into how the Chinese armed forces operate and what their current capabilities are.[27] The export of technologically advanced weapon systems could then be regulated accordingly, thereby ensuring Russia maintains the technological edge over China. Table 4.1 outlines Russian military sales to China from 1999 to 2006:

---

24   Blank, 'China-Taiwan Arms Race Quickens'.
25   'Annual Report to Congress: Military Power of the People's Republic of China 2006', p. 21.
26   Blank, 'China-Taiwan Arms Race Quickens'.
27   de Haas, 'Russian-Chinese military exercises and their wider perspective: Power play in Central Asia', p. 5.

Table 4.1: Deliveries of Russian military equipment to the PRC from 1999 to 2006

Armament	Designation	Producer	Delivery	Quantity	Remarks
Weapons for Air Forces					
Fighter	Su-27SK	Sukhoi Design Bureau, Komsomolsk-on-Amur Aviation Production Plant	2006	c.110	Licensed production at Shenyang
Trainer-Fighter	Su-27UBK	NPK Irkut	1992-02	40	
Multi-role Fighter	Su-30MKK	Komsomolsk-on-Amur Aviation Production Plant	2000-03	72	
Multi-role Fighter	Su-30MKK	Komsomolsk-on-Amur Aviation Production Plant	2000-03	72	
Transport/ Tanker	Il-76/Il-78	Ilyushin Aviation Production Plant	2007-08	34/4	
Weapons for Naval Forces					
Diesel-Electric Submarine	Project 636	Admiralty Shipyard, Krasnaye Sormovo, Sevmash Plant	2005-06	8	All units are to be equipped with Klub (SS-N-27 ASCM)
Destroyer	Project 956EM	Severnoe PKB, Severnaya Shipyard	1999, 2000, 2006	6	Latter two destroyers come with more advanced weapon systems
Multi-role Naval Fighter	Su-30MK2	Sukhoi, Komsomolsk-on-Amur Aviation Production Plant	2004	24	An order for a second batch is probable for 2006
Onboard SAM System	S-300F (SA-N-6 Grumble)	NPO Al'tair Design Bureau	2002	2	Probably for a Project 052S destroyer
Onboard SAM System	Shtil'-1 (SA-N-7 Gauntlet)	Concern PVO-Almaz Antei	Probably 2003	Probably 2	For a Project 052B destroyer
Weapons and Military Equipment for Anti-Air Defense					
Long-Range SAM System	S-300P (SA-10 Grumble)	Concern PVO	1998-04	12 batteries	
Long-Range SAM System	S-300PMU-2 (SA-20 Gargoyle)	Concern PVO	Before 2007	16 batteries	
Short-Range SAM System	Tor-M1 (SA-15 Gauntlet)	Concern Antei, State Enterprise Kupol Izhevsk	?	27 systems	

(**Source: Moscow Defense Brief,** Centre for Analysis and Strategic Technologies, available at <http://mdb.cast.ru>, accessed 6 February 2007)

After examining the weapons sold to China, it is clear that air and naval weaponry has accounted for the vast bulk of Russian arms exports. This trend highlights China's intention to upgrade its power projection capabilities, thereby enhancing control over its maritime approaches and, if necessary, its ability to act in response to a Taiwan contingency. The deployment of the various air, naval and missile assets along the coastline opposite Taiwan is testament to this strategy, as is China's likely contract for six Zubr (*Pomornik*) heavy-assault hovercraft from Russia[28]—perfect assets for a Taiwan invasion. Old Chinese concerns over land borders have been discarded in favour of seeking air and naval supremacy over China's east and southeast. This is reflected in its procurement plans, which have shifted away from seemingly endless production runs of clunky armour, infantry weapons and other 1960s weaponry to more sophisticated air and naval assets, both domestic and Russian.[29] This has helped to allay Moscow's concerns over Chinese intentions, as Beijing's focus is now apparently on geographic regions devoid of Russian interests. This in turn has also helped to sustain the level of bilateral trade for arms, and may even be a factor behind the provision of more advanced Russian weapon systems for export to China.

Future Prospects

The warming of Sino-Russian relations post SCO and *Peace Mission 2005* has meant Russia's option to sell more advanced weapon systems to China is looking increasingly realistic. Beijing's intensified efforts to modernise its armed forces is resulting in rapid increases in defence expenses and currently makes China the main strategic partner for Russia in military-technical cooperation. According to Russian defence industry expert Konstantin Makienko, China will continue focusing its efforts on improving its Air Force and Navy:

> The main objective in aviation is the modernization of the fleet of Su-27SK and J-11 aircraft. It would be most reasonable if these aircraft are upgraded to the Su-27SKM version, but it is also quite possible that far less reserved variants of modernization will be provided, including with integration of phased array radars.[30]

In terms of naval equipment, the most likely future transfer from Russia to China is more advanced air defence missile systems. Furthermore, Russia may assist the Chinese Navy in enhancing its amphibious capabilities, allowing licence-production of Zubr (*Pomornik*) or *Murena-E* assault hovercraft to

---

28　'China to but 540t Zubr class assault hovercraft', *Military Procurement International*, vol. 16, no. 19, 1 October 2006, p. 1.

29　Bates Gill, 'China's Newest Warships', *Far Eastern Economic Review*, 27 January 2000, p. 30.

30　Konstantin Makienko, in 'China to Remain Russia's Main Arms Market—Expert', 20 March 2006, available at <http://www.mosnews.com>, accessed 25 March 2006.

complement the six Zubrs likely to be signed for in 2007. However, the largest cooperation project may involve Russia assisting China in building its desired aircraft carrier fleet. The main contribution Russia can make to this project is to allow licence-production in China of the Su-30 *Flanker* navalised variant, the Su-33.[31] If they come to fruition, these options are significant for two reasons. First, they would indicate that Russia does not fear a military threat to its own interests from China, at least in the near term. Second, the bulk of recent and potential future arms sales have involved air and naval weapons that would be required in any clash between China and the United States over Taiwan, but are of little use to China in a future war with Russia.

The next decade or so will likely see a continuation of the trends of the last decade; that is, significant Chinese business for Russian arms manufacturers. China will probably continue to purchase Russian naval, air, and air-defence systems from Russia in an effort to fill niche gaps in capability and to make up for deficiencies in its indigenous production lines. However, as Chinese technologies develop, and Chinese satisfaction in receiving second-tier military hardware from Russia dwindles, Russia will risk losing a key customer. Often discussed in the Western press, the potential removal of the European Union's arms embargo from China will have no less of a negative impact on Russian sales than Chinese defence industrial advancement. In fact, the majority of Chinese arms trade experts agree that, in general, EU expansion into the Chinese market poses only a very minor threat to Russia's position. The Europeans have a competitive position only in those sectors where Russia has nothing of significance to offer, namely communications, optical-electronic and laser-based systems.[32]

The Sino-Russian military technical nexus is alive and well. Despite the inherent risks to these traditional adversaries within the relationship, both sides are also managing to derive tangible benefits. China is receiving new weapon systems faster than it could without Russian assistance, as well as slowly mastering a great deal of new Russian-sourced military technology. Russia is receiving not only the finance to assist the development of its OPK but also the orders of military equipment that are required to keep many military production lines operating. This position will probably remain for the next decade. The downside for Russia is that there is an increasing chance that China will catch up technologically and lower its demand for Russian arms. If this does occur, it will be beyond the next decade, by which time a combination of Russia's own domestic orders and the Rosoboronexport sales drive into the Middle East, Latin America and Southeast Asia will have compensated for the contraction in the Chinese market. Considering the 2006 US$3 billion and US$7.5 billion arms

---

31   Makienko, in 'China to Remain Russia's Main Arms Market—Expert'.
32   Makienko, 'The Russian-Chinese Arms Trade: an Attempt at Qualitative Analysis'.

orders from Venezuela and Algeria respectively, Russia seems well on the way to compensating for the potential future loss of its traditionally most prized arms customer.

Chapter 5
External Drivers for OPK Success: Arms Transfers to India

Russia has sold weapons worth over 10bn dollars to India over the last five years and contracts worth another US$9 billion dollars are currently being worked on.[1]

Aleksandr Zhukov, March 2006

India's choice of Russian military hardware is determined by a host of factors, such as their easy accessibility, the defence requirements of India's armed forces, the quality of weapons, and pricing considerations. It is no secret that Russia sells similar weaponry at half the price demanded by European countries.[2] For example, a Russian *Kilo*-class diesel-electric submarine currently costs around US$200 million, whilst the less capable German Type 209 diesel-electric submarine costs around US$450 million. The Indian Navy operates 10 *Kilo*-class submarines but only four Type 209 submarines. A further factor is the inertia created by India's four decades of heavy dependence on Russian military hardware. India's strategic analysts have argued a case against this reliance, pointing out that India must diversify its sources of weapons procurement because of the threat associated with reliance upon a single supplier. However, these warnings continue to go unheeded by the Indian Government, which retains its preference for Russian equipment. According to Western sources, signed deals and prepared future transactions in defence procurement between Russia and India for the next 8–10 years were estimated to be at least US$12 billion. This was in 2003. After Vladimir Putin's late 2004 visit to India, the expected sum of the contracts for arms destined for India over the next 15 years skyrocketed to US$30 billion.[3] By 2004 about 40 per cent of Russian military exports were destined for India. For the next 20 years New Delhi plans to allocate about US$100 billion for the procurement of military hardware, and the Russians will most likely receive the lion's share of this figure.

An Indo-Russian defence accord, set to expire in 2010, was extended for a further ten years. This was decided at the fifth meeting of the Indo-Russian Inter-Governmental Commission on military-technical cooperation in November 2005.

---

1   Aleksandr Zhukov, in 'Russia boosts military and technical cooperation with *India'*, *India* Daily, 16 March 2006, available at <http://www.indiadaily.com/editorial/7453.asp>, accessed 28 April 2009.

2   B.M. Jain, 'India and Russia: Reassessing the time tested ties', *Pacific Affairs,* vol. 76, no. 3, Fall 2003, p. 384.

3   Alister Maunk, 'Military Cooperation of Russia and India In 1991–2005', 3 June 2005, available at <http://www.axisglobe.com/article.asp?article=140>, accessed 28 April 2009.

Indian Defence Minister Pranab Mukherjee stated at this meeting that Russia would continue to assist Indian shipyards, as it did in April 2005, with the laying down of the 37 500 tonne aircraft carrier (Air-Defence Ship or ADS) at Cochin Shipyard. As an aside, India has no indigenous carrier-based aircraft and so will probably exercise its option to procure another 30 MiG-29K navalised *Fulcrum* aircraft for this new aircraft carrier to complement the 16 it has already ordered for the *Admiral Gorshkov*.

India has also entered into an agreement to lease two Russian *Akula II* nuclear attack submarines to develop the sea leg of its three-tier strategic deterrent. The first boat underwent sea-trials in the Russian Far East and was expected to enter service sometime in 2008. Mukherjee also told a press conference in Moscow that India would join Russia in developing and financing a fifth-generation fighter aircraft project, as well as agreeing to utilise the Russian Glonass navigational satellite system, an alternative to the US-controlled Global Positioning System.[4] India's preference to source strategic systems such as nuclear submarines and satellite systems from Russia is due to the fact that it has few sourcing options for such systems and its perception that Russia is a reliable provider unlikely to impose sanctions for political or human rights indiscretions.

Moscow seems to be more relaxed about offering military technologies to India than to China. An idea of the staggering Russian influence on Indian defence procurement is provided by the fact that about 60 per cent of the Indian Army's military hardware is Russian-made, while 70 per cent of naval systems and 80 per cent of air force hardware is Russian-made or of Russian origin. Overall, 70 per cent of the military hardware in the Indian armed forces comes from Russia.[5] In this light, it is easy to see why India will remain a key market for Russian arms well into the future. Russia has sold over US\$10 billion worth of weapons to India between 2001 and 2006 and contracts worth another US\$9 billion are currently under consideration.[6] This will ensure that India remains a key customer well into the next decade.

Indeed, Russia's presence within India's defence industries is almost omnipresent, with licence-production of Russian designed tanks and aircraft in the form of 1000 T-90 MBTs, 140 Su-30MKI fighters, and 64 MiG-29SMT fighters. Indian warships currently under construction also have a Russian influence due to the presence of Russian advisors and engineers within the Indian shipyards. These vessels range from an aircraft carrier, air-defence destroyers and frigates, to nuclear submarines. When complete, many of these vessels will incorporate Russian designed and developed missile and radar systems. Notable direct sales

---

4   Rahul Bedi, 'India, Russia to renew accord for 10 more years', *Jane's Defence Weekly*, 30 November 2005.
5   I. Dimitryev, 'Hello to Arms', *Versiya*, no. 19, 22–28 May 2006, p. 9.
6   Aleksandr Zhukov, in 'Russia: Over \$10 billion worth of weapons exported to India', Press Conference, *Interfax*, 16 March 2006.

over the last few years have included six *Talwar* frigates to compensate for the slow delivery of Indian platforms, as well as *Smerch* multiple launch rocket systems, and *Tunguska* air defence systems to compensate for the problems inherent within India land defence industries.

India's traditional reliance on Russian hardware has meant that revenues continue to flow well after the last piece of hardware has been sold. For example, Russia has been upgrading India's 1960s and 1970s fleet of MiG-21 *Fishbed* and MiG-27 *Flogger* D fighter and ground-attack aircraft over the last five years, which could potentially net Russia US$800 million. As previously discussed, Indo-Russian relations are not, however, narrowly confined to a 'buyer-seller relationship'. They have gone beyond that stage and show that the two nations trust each other, as evidenced in their joint design and production of weapons such as *BrahMos* ASCM.[7] Table 5.1 is a summary of key Russian arms contracts with India since 1999:

Table 5.1: Key Russian Arms Contracts with India from 1999

Contract	Price	Delivery	Notes
Admiral Gorshkov aircraft-carrier equipment package	$1.6bn	2008	Cost is for overhaul and upgrade, and the delivery of 16 MiG-29Ks.
Construction of three Talwar frigates	$1bn	2004	The first two, the Talwar and the Trishul, delivered in 2003.
8 Su-30K and 32 Su-30MKI fighters		2004	
6 Il-78 MIDAS air tankers	$150m	2003	
310 T-90S tanks	$800m	2003	124 tanks delivered, and 186 licence produced in India.
5 Ka-31RLD helicopters	$108m	2002	
Upgrade of 5 Il-38 MAY anti-submarine aircraft for the Indian Navy	$205m	2007	Upgrade involves the installation of Sea Dragon radar system.
40 Mi-17 helicopters	$170m	2001	
Licensed production of 140 Su-30MKI in India	$3bn	2012–2017	
Several hundred Igla MANPADs	$32m	2001	
1000 Krasnopol-M laser-guided artillery shells	$35m	2000	
Construction of three Talwar frigates	$1.1bn	2012	

---

7   G. Fernandes in, B.M. Jain, 'India and Russia: Reassessing the time tested ties', *Pacific Affairs*, vol. 76, no. 3, Fall 2003, p. 385.

Contract	Price	Delivery	Notes
36 Smerch multiple launch Rocket Systems, with rockets	$500m	2007	
Upgrade of 66 MiG-29 Fulcrum	c.$890m	c.2011	
License production of 1000 T-90S tanks		c.2020	Deliveries over the next 15 years.
Fitting-out and leasing of two Akula II nuclear submarines	c.$1.8bn	2007–08	First hull currently being readied for sea trials.
24 Tunguska-M1 air-defence systems	$400m	2007	
140 RD-33 aero-engines	$250m	2007	120 for license production for the MiG-29 upgrade. Could give Russia advantage in c.$9bn Indian tender for 126 multi-role fighters.
Mi-17 1V helicopters	c.$662m	2007–08	

(*Sources: Moscow Defense Brief*, Centre for Analysis and Strategic Technologies, available at <http://mdb. cast.ru>, accessed 12 February 2007, *Jane's Defence Weekly*, and <http://www.mosnews.com/money>, accessed 12 February 2007)

Historical Basis

Since the early 1950s, New Delhi and Moscow have built friendly relations on the basis of *realpolitik*. India's nonalignment policy enabled it to accept Soviet support in areas of strategic congruence such as disputes with Pakistan and China, without subscribing to Soviet global policies or proposals for Asian collective security.[8] The most intimate phase in relations between India and the Soviet Union was between 1971 and 1976. This phase was characterised by the 20-year *Treaty of Peace, Friendship, and Cooperation* of August 1971, which committed the parties 'to abstain from providing any assistance to any third party that engages in armed conflict with the other' and 'in the event of either party being subjected to an attack or threat thereof … to immediately enter into mutual consultations'. This Treaty led the Soviet Union to support the Indian position on Bangladesh, to India's benefit, and acted as a deterrent to Chinese involvement within the dispute.[9] By the late 1970s, the Soviet Union became India's largest trading partner.

Upon the disintegration of the Soviet Union, India was faced with the difficult task of reorienting its external affairs and forging relations with the 15 Soviet

---

8   Rouben Azizian, 'Russia-India Relations: Stability amidst Strategic Uncertainty', *Special Assessment: Asia's Bilateral Relations*, Asia-Pacific Center for Security Studies, Honolulu, October 2004, p. 3, available at <http://www.apcss.org/Publications/SAS/AsiaBilateralRelations/Russia-IndiaRelationsAzizian.pdf>, accessed 28 April 2009.

9   Azizian, 'Russia-India Relations: Stability amidst Strategic Uncertainty', p. 3.

successor states, of which Russia was the most important. Russia's first government made relations with the United States and the West its priority and it expressed diminished interest in Asia, signaling a strong will to distance itself from the legacy of Soviet foreign policy.

Russia's foreign policy, however, soon reverted from the idealism of the early 1990s to traditional *realpolitik*, which prompted urgent diplomatic efforts to repair the damage in relations with India. President Boris Yeltsin's visit to India in January 1993 laid the foundation for the reinvigoration of bilateral relations. Yeltsin expressed strong support for India's position on Kashmir and pledged not to provide arms to Pakistan. Yeltsin signed a defence cooperation accord aimed at ensuring the continued supply of Russian arms and spare parts in order to satisfy the requirements of India's military and to promote the joint production of defense equipment.[10] The Russian Prime Minister at the time, Yevgeny Primakov, visited New Delhi in December 1998, resulting in the formation of seven agreements with the Indian Government. One of the agreements was a long-term military cooperation pact until 2010, and was of particular importance. Commitment to the agreements has since been reaffirmed by both states. Indian Defence Minister Pranab Mukherjee has stated: 'After 2010 we will review the progress and have another 10-year programme. Our defence cooperation with Russia is a continuous process and some projects will overlap the 2010 threshold.'[11]

In March 1999, India and Russia signed a further agreement to train Indian defence personnel in key Russian military academies. These actions set the platform for continued Indo-Russian cooperation throughout the 1990s and into the early twenty-first century. In turn, four more major agreements in the field of defence were signed in New Delhi on 4 October 2000. The agreements were significantly concluded against the background of the visit of President Vladimir Putin and the signing of the *Declaration on Strategic Partnership* between India and Russia.

Of these four agreements signed in October 2000, the first relates to the establishment of the Indo-Russian Inter-governmental Commission on Military Technical Cooperation, signed by then Indian Defence Minister George Fernandes and Russian Deputy Prime Minister Ilya Klebanov. The Commission meets annually and has under it two Working Groups, the first one dealing with military-technical cooperation and the second with defence production in the fields of shipbuilding, aviation and land systems. It exercises coordination and

---

10   Azizian, 'Russia-India Relations: Stability amidst Strategic Uncertainty', p. 3.

11   Indian Defence Minister Pranab Mukherjee, in Vladimir Radyuhin, 'India, Russia to Renew Defense Programme', *The Hindu*, 18 November 2005, available at <http://www.hinduonnet.com/2005/11/18/stories/2005111817131400.htm>, accessed 28 April 2009.

control of bilateral military-technical cooperation, facilitates its development, resolves problems emerging in the course of implementation of military-technical cooperation, and assists in accelerating decision-making.[12]

The important feature of the long-term military-technical cooperation agreement was that it covered new areas of mutual cooperation such as naval and nuclear technologies and anti-ballistic missile systems.[13] It paved the way for enhancing the joint research and development (R&D) capabilities of India and Russia in the production of new weapon systems, leading, in the first instance, to the production of the *BrahMos* ASCM. The successful co-production of *BrahMos* has further propelled New Delhi and Moscow to co-develop a fifth-generation fighter aircraft. In this way, the defence relationship is set to further deepen in the years ahead and subsequently expand the existing ties between Russia and India,[14] most probably in the form of more military joint ventures, continued arms contracts and ongoing Indian military personnel training in Russia. The remaining three agreements were specifically related to military platforms and covered delivery and license production of Su-30MKI aircraft, the refit and delivery of the *Admiral Gorshkov* carrier with supporting MiG-29K aircraft, and the delivery of 310 T-90 MBTs.

As stated by Indo-Russian relations expert Rouben Azizian: 'The January 1993 Treaty of Friendship and Cooperation and the October 2000 Declaration on Strategic Partnership serve as the two guiding documents of the Post-Cold War Russo-Indian partnership.'[15]

These documents state that the partnership between Russia and India is founded on complementary national interests and geopolitical priorities. For example, 'Russia's high standing as a world power' and India's leading role in the 'immediate neighborhood, in Asia and beyond', display the complementary natures of the two states.[16] Moscow continues to consider South Asia as an Indian dominated domain and openly supports India's bid for permanent membership on the United Nations Security Council. Meanwhile, India uses its growing input into the SCO to lend support to Russia's pre-eminent role in the former Soviet states, particularly in Central Asia. This way, Russia and India support each other's sphere of influence and maintain healthy relations with one another.

In 2004 the Russian Federation appointed a new ambassador, Vyacheslav Trubnikov, to India. His credentials were impressive: an ex-director of Russian

---

12 'India and Russia sign four defence agreements', 2001, available at <http://mod.nic.in/samachar/nov15-20/html/ch16.htm>, accessed 28 April 2009.
13 Jain, 'India and Russia: Reassessing the time tested ties', *Pacific Affairs*, vol. 76, no. 3, Fall 2003, p. 382.
14 'India and Russia sign four defence agreements'
15 Azizian, 'Russia-India Relations: Stability amidst Strategic Uncertainty', p. 3.
16 Azizian, 'Russia-India Relations: Stability amidst Strategic Uncertainty', p. 4.

special services, a former Deputy Minister of Foreign Affairs, colleague and confidant of Yevgeny Primakov, and one of the leading experts on Hindustan. Trubnikov's appointment as Russian ambassador to India was a sign of the importance that Moscow devoted to relations with New Delhi.[17]

Military sales form the keystone of the Indo-Russia relationship. From 1990–96, India's arms purchases from Russia totaled US$3.5 billion. During this period, Russia committed itself to supplying India with 50 Su-30 multifunctional fighters and agreed that an Indian enterprise could produce a modified version of the plane under licence. The modified Su-30 became the Su-30MKI—a very capable platform boasting Western avionics, thrust-vectoring engines, and canards to assist in dog-fighting capabilities. By the end of 1999, the strength of Indo-Russian military cooperation had returned to its Cold War level, with all three branches of the Indian military involved in major procurement programs with Russia. Of paramount concern for Indian naval planners was the requirement for a new ADS to replace the INS *Vikrant*—one of two former British light aircraft carriers owned by India that was decommissioned in 1997. The Indian Navy, with almost 85 per cent of its vessels of Soviet-Russian origin, was quick to rejuvenate the sagging Indo-Russian bond. To fill the gap in capability between the decommissioning of the *Vikrant* and the commissioning of the ADS, India acquired the 44 500 tonne *Admiral Gorshkov* aircraft carrier from Russia, which is to be renamed the INS *Vikramaditya* and commissioned in 2010.[18] In conjunction with the delivery of the three *Talwar* frigates between 2001 and 2004 and the subsequent contract signed in 2006 for three more, it is evident that India lacks the construction capacity and ability to meet the construction timelines necessary to replace ageing Soviet-supplied ships. Therefore, with the delivery of more Russian built vessels, the Indo-Russian naval bond will remain for several more decades.[19]

While India maintains a vast pool of engineering and scientific knowledge, its defence industry habitually struggles in its attempts to coordinate the various research elements involved in a project's development. This shortcoming in project management is exacerbated by the absence of market-based efficiency since India's Defence Research and Development Organisation provides the primary R&D for all of India's indigenous military projects. Technical and financial considerations mean that very few countries are able to develop and field completely indigenous weapon systems. So, while India is still forced to rely on external support for many of its indigenous projects, it continues to simultaneously promote the idea of self-reliance. The tension resulting from

---

17   Maunk, 'Military Cooperation of Russia and India In 1991–2005'.

18   Jerome M. Conley, *Indo-Russian Military and Nuclear Cooperation*, Lexington Books, Lanham, MD, 2001, p. 69.

19   Conley, *Indo-Russian Military and Nuclear Cooperation*, p. 70.

heavy reliance on external support and the failures of project management is highlighted by one of India's most publicised and criticised indigenous projects: the *Arjun* MBT,[20] which has been in development for over 25 years, and continues to be plagued with mechanical faults. In response to Pakistan's procurement of the T-80UD MBT from the Ukraine, and its inability to field the *Arjun* MBT, India turned yet again to Russia for an interim capability. Russia offered the T-90S MBT, and 310 were delivered by 2004, with a further 690 to be licence-produced from 2007.[21] The Indian Government has called for the remaining Indian T-72 MBT fleet to be upgraded, and as the preferred supplier, Russia looks set to gain more Indian business at the expense of the unfortunate Indian *Arjun* indigenous tank program. The far more capable T-90S cost the Indians US$2.4 million each, and was ready when required, whilst the *Arjun* cost US$5.3 million each.[22] India remains unable to rapidly progress in the development of its indigenous military production. As one retired Indian army officer stated: 'No country, however wealthy, can afford to produce three different tanks simultaneously.'[23]

The *Arjun* tanks may be shelved permanently due to these issues, and a contract for yet another 330 T-90S kits was signed in October 2006 for US$600 million,[24] suggesting that the Indian Army could be moving towards an exclusive T-72/T-90S MBT fleet. Furthermore, at the seventh meeting of the Indo-Russian Inter-Governmental Commission on Military-Technical Cooperation, it was agreed to co-develop a next generation MBT based on Russia's highly secretive T-95. This will ensure that India maintains its MBT edge over its rivals well into the twenty-first century.

The previously discussed Indo-Russian reaffirmation of their commitment to continued military cooperation in October 2000 occurred despite the apprehension of some Indian policy-makers about the modernisation of the Indian military and the ongoing heavy reliance on Russia to usher in this modernisation. Russia's interest in maintaining its crucial arms market presence in India led it to present India with a unique lease agreement for two *Akula II* nuclear attack submarines and four Tupolev Tu-22M *Backfire* strategic bombers, of which only the submarine lease has been officially agreed upon. Despite Indian reticence to accept the *Backfire* lease, the Indian Air Force continues to fly a predominantly Russian aircraft fleet. The large number of MiG and Sukhoi aircraft makes continued Indo-Russian cooperation in this field highly likely.

---

20   Conley, *Indo-Russian Military and Nuclear Cooperation*, p. 66.
21   'Army to acquire nearly 1000 additional T90 tanks by 2020', 4 October 2006, available at <http://www.india-defence.com/reports/2577>, accessed 28 April 2009.
22   Conley, *Indo-Russian Military and Nuclear Cooperation*, p. 72.
23   Conley, *Indo-Russian Military and Nuclear Cooperation*, p. 72.
24   'India Buys 330 Russian Tanks', *MosNews*, 27 October 2006, available at <http://www.defenceindia.com/23-oct-2k6/news15.html>, accessed 28 April 2009.

International Policy Considerations

Indian international policy advisors reiterate India's need to realise full cooperative potential with Russia and to develop relations to the fullest extent. They advocate that India is an almost perfect military-industrial partner for Russia.[25] Compared to China, the Indo-Russian relationship is practically void of military-political complications and Russia's extensive history of joint projects with India holds it in good stead for future cooperation. Speaking in Russia during a high profile visit in December 2005 that focused on an intellectual property rights agreement Indian Prime Minister Manmohan Singh stated that:

> Our perspective … is to move towards collaborative projects involving design, development and production of the next generation military products. India and Russia have identified the medium-range transport aircraft and the fifth-generation fighter aircraft as two such projects.[26]

The agreement regarding intellectual property rights has opened the doors to large-scale cooperation between their respective armed forces and defence industries. During the 2005 meeting, Putin and Singh affirmed their commitment to continue to foster defence cooperation by describing it as 'a vital pillar' of Indo-Russian strategic partnership and another manifestation of deep mutual trust and commonality of interests between the two states.[27] It would seem, therefore, that the concerns aired by some Indian defence officials regarding the reliance of the armed forces on Russian platforms are unfounded, as the two states appear to be moving down similar strategic paths. The reliance is seemingly reciprocal, as opposed to one-sided, as Russia requires the Indian arms market as a customer as much as India requires Russian military equipment as a supplier.

India was placed under a US arms embargo from 1998, following Indian nuclear tests. The lifting of this embargo in 2001 saw the potential for US competition within the Indian arms market. Russia, therefore, sought to secure as many agreements with India as possible: hence the 10-year deals. In particular, Russia has endeavoured to streamline the acquisition process for parts, with the creation of Rosoboronservice, a Rosoboronexport subsidiary that is based in India with a mandate to repair Russian-sourced military equipment. Russian arms manufacturers also hope to wield the lower costs of their products as a marketing tool against the more expensive US weapons. Finally, Russia has

---

25 Maunk, 'Military Cooperation of Russia and India In 1991–2005'.

26 Indian Prime Minister Mammohan Singh, in 'India, Russia to Develop New Generation Weapons Together—Indian PM', *MosNews*, 6 December 2005, available at <http://engforum.pravda.ru/archive/index.php/t-152220.html>, accessed 28 April 2009.

27 'Indian Russia leaders see military, technical ties as 'vital pillar'', New Delhi PTI News Agency, 7 December 2005.

offered to export highly sophisticated technology to India, including non-lethal microwave-beam weapons, and to sell advanced air-defence systems that can counteract the proposed US missile-defence shield.[28]

From a military perspective, the Russian relationship with India is one that the United States cannot hope to match. Washington found itself in a quandary during its embargo of India following the latter's 1998 nuclear tests. The predicament was that the Indo-Russian arms connection could only be severed by the United States through counteroffers of third-party arms (because of the US arms embargo on India) or by the slow emergence of Indian military self-sufficiency. Even with the lifting of the US embargo, India remains heavily reliant upon Russian sourced weapon systems and its indigenous production will continue to be far from providing self-sufficiency over the next decade at least. For the foreseeable future, it is Russia, not the United States, which will hold the premier source of Indian arms status—a role it has held since the 1960s. It seems that the United States may have missed the opportunity to forge an Indo-American relationship as strong and interdependent as the Indo-Russian relationship.

Future Prospects

The Indian market [for arms] will remain capacious enough for Russia at least as long as we live.[29]

Russian Defence Minister Sergei Ivanov's statement is a strong indication of where the prospects for Indo-Russian arms transfers are headed into the future. In the near term, India's Chief of Air Force, Shashindra Pal Tyagi, announced India's intention to buy 80 Mi-17 utility helicopters from Russia, with a contract signed in October 2006. The deal was estimated at US$662 million.[30] However, by far the biggest request for tender in the history of the Indian armed forces is the much anticipated requirement for 126 multi-role combat aircraft, estimated to cost between US$7 and US$11 billion. The Indian Government should make a decision on the choice of aircraft in 2009, and the highly maneuverable and significantly upgraded MiG-29 variant, the MiG-35 *Fulcrum,* is tipped to be one of the favourites. Supporting its chances is the fact that the Indian Air Force already has 66 in its inventory and the Indian Navy will be receiving the navalised variant for the carrier operations. The biggest boost for MiG, however,

---

28   Tom Lansford, 'US-Russian Rivalry in the Arms Trade of South Asia', *Security Dialogue,* vol. 33, no. 2, June 2002, p. 135.

29   Sergei Ivanov in, 'Russian-Indian commission to address promising projects in military-technical cooperation', Press Release, *Interfax,* 14 November 2005.

30   Alexandra Gritskova and Konstantin Lantratov, 'Russian Mi-17 to land in India', *Kommersant,* 11 July 2006, p. 10.

came in September 2006, when India signed a contract to licence-produce the MiG power plant—the RD-33 engine. As one of the stipulations for the fighter contract is licence-production in India, the fact that it will already be producing the power plants could tip the scales in favour of the MiG tender.

In the longer term, India has indicated a preference for MiG as the producer of its joint fifth-generation fighter. This is an interesting development, as the Russian Government backed the Sukhoi's PAK-FA fifth-generation fighter. However Indian defence officials have stated that this aircraft is too heavy for their requirements: hence the MiG preference. Defence Minister Pranab Mukherjee publicly acknowledged that India was keen to take part in the development and financing of a MiG fifth-generation fighter with Russia during his November 2005 visit to Moscow.[31] Half of the financing will be provided by India, in return for joint production rights and potentially technology transfer. MiG's booming sales through very large orders from India, Yemen and Algeria in the last year would suggest that it may have enough funds to finance the remaining half of the project even without Russian governmental assistance. This would suggest that, in the long-term, Russia will have two fifth-generation fighters (medium and heavy) at its disposal—an unaffordable luxury prior to India's decision to help fund the MiG project. The PAK-FA and MiG projects will likely replace the Su-27/30 and MiG-29/35 families respectively, once they reach initial operating capability.

Furthermore, the comprehensive agreement for the creation of the medium transport aircraft (MTA) occurred in January 2007. The MTA would be designed, developed and manufactured jointly and would fulfill airlift requirements for both the Russian and Indian Air Forces. The aircraft is designed to replace Russia and India's An-12 *Cub*, An-24 *Coke* and An-32 *Curl* medium transports. Russia recently reneged on its obligations to a joint project with the Ukraine for a similar transport aircraft. This action is an indication of the importance that Russia is placing on the MTA, now the favoured future transport aircraft for Russian requirements and due to make its maiden flight in 2012.[32] In terms of land systems, India is interested in acquiring the potent S-300 *Grumble/Gargoyle* theatre air defence unit to complement the short and medium range systems already purchased from Russia. There is also talk of a contract for the upgrade of India's T-72 fleet of MBTs to complement the licensed production of the T-90S MBT.

---

31   'Mukherjee invites RAC MiG to present concept of fifth-gen plane', 2005, available at <http://www.outlookindia.com>, accessed 12 December 2006.

32   'Russia, India may sign military transport plane deal in August', RIA Novosti, 1 August 2007, available at <http://www.globalsecurity.org/wmd/library/news/india/2007/india-070801-rianovosti01.htm>, accessed 28 April 2009.

As highlighted by the 2005 meetings in Moscow, India will continue to procure traditional weapon systems from Russia, such as tanks, heavy artillery and aircraft, and will collaborate in further joint ventures for at least the next decade. Until India is able to secure a reliable indigenous production base for its military needs, and unless other suppliers of major weapon systems are willing to offer India licensing rights as well as end items, India's reliance upon Russia as a weaponry provider will persist.[33] Future Indo-Russian ties are likely to meet with greater success, especially in the strategic defence field, as the two states currently have no direct conflict of interest. Their defence ties are not restricted to the mere buyer-seller relationship but are, more significantly, expanding and deepening in terms of co-production of state-of-the-art weaponry. Their approaches to vital strategic issues such as the multipolar world structure, counter-terrorism and the development of nuclear technology cooperation will serve to further solidify their ties.[34]

33   Conley, *Indo-Russian Military and Nuclear Cooperation*, p. 74.
34   Jain, 'India and Russia: Reassessing the time tested ties', *Pacific Affairs*, vol. 76, no. 3, Fall 2003, p. 396.

Chapter 6
External Drivers for OPK Success: Emerging Markets

Other than the lucrative Indian and Chinese markets, there are a number of other markets that have been cultivated by the Putin Administration since 2000. With widespread expectations that the Chinese market in particular will begin to level out within the next 5–10 years, concerted marketing drives have been made into the Middle East, Southeast Asia, and Latin America by Rosoboronexport and the leading Russian defence enterprises. These efforts are beginning to pay dividends, as major arms contracts in 2006 signed by Algeria and Venezuela are expected to trigger further exports in these regions. As for Southeast Asia, a Russian offer of a US$1 billion export credit for arms was accepted by Indonesia in December 2006, and ratified in September 2007. This agreement, in conjunction with other Russian arms sales to China, Myanmar, and Malaysia, bodes well for future Russian arms exports to Southeast Asia.

While the sheer volume of Russian arms sales is a clear economic indicator, it also demonstrates the extent of Russia's growing influence around the world. Recent arms deals show that Russia is building on its former influence in the Middle East, and forging ahead in the relatively untapped markets of Southeast Asia and Latin America. These markets have not only conducted business with Rosoboronexport, but also with individual manufacturers such as Sukhoi and RSK MiG. In 2005, Russia sold weapons to 61 countries, some of which are now challenging the likes of India and China in terms of financial recompense for Russia.[1] Both the Venezuelan and Algerian contracts were multi-billion dollar affairs, showing that Russia's market diversification efforts are now beginning to pay handsome dividends.

Russia's foreign order book for arms had reached approximately US$20 billion by the time of publication. Alexander Fomin, Deputy Director of the Russian Federation Military-Technical Service, indicated that actual sales were likely to reach US$8.5 billion in 2009. This would account for 40 per cent of the workload of Russia's *Oboronnyi-promyshennyi kompleks* (OPK) and he suggested that defence industries would be able to manage this demand comfortably.[2]

---

1   Victor Yasmann, 'Russia: Putin Pushes Greater Arms Exports', 4 April 2006, available at <http://www.globalsecurity.org/wmd/library/news/russia/2006/russia-060404-rferl01.htm>, accessed 28 April 2009.
2   'Russia Optimistically Targeting $8.5 Billion in Arms Exports in 2009', *Defence Talk*, 17 February 2009, available at <http://www.defencetalk.com/russia-optimistically-targeting-85-billion-in-arms-exports-in-2009-16578/>, accessed 7 December 2009; and Nikolai Novichkov, 'Russian defence exports surpass targets', *Jane's Defence Industry*, 1 March 2006.

Vladimir Putin maintains a keen interest in Russian arms sales around the world and to date has successfully lobbied for the sale of weapon systems during visits to Algeria, Libya, Malaysia, Thailand, South Korea, Turkey and several other Middle Eastern countries.[3] Key to this diversification success has been the efforts in recent years by Putin, Sergei Ivanov, and indeed ex-Rosoboronexport chief, Sergei Chemezov, to provide more flexible and creative financing and payment options for prospective arms clients. This has been a major contributing factor to the recent boom in arms sales. As stated by Richard Grimmett in his report to the US Congress regarding arms transfers to developing nations, the Russians have

> agreed to engage in counter trade [with China], offsets [with Malaysia], debt-swapping [with South Korea], and in key cases [China and India], to make significant licensed production agreements in order to sell it weapons.[4]

This flexibility, coupled with an export drive focused on market diversification has not only increased sales but also expanded the market. In 2002 the geography of cooperation of the world arms market included 30 countries, but, according to Ivanov, as of January 2006 Russia was exporting arms to 82 countries.[5]

Moreover, the Russian export credit offer of US$1 billion was formally accepted by Indonesia in December 2006. Such credit offers represent yet another funding option that Russia can offer its arms clients in the future. This flexible financing policy, in conjunction with its liberal export policy, (it rarely lets political considerations such as those related to human rights or 'rogue states' affect its export policies) makes Russia a more attractive option as an arms source than the United States for many countries around the world.

Assisting Russia's booming arms export receipts are economic and political developments within three of the world's geopolitical regions. In the Middle East, the steady rise in the price of oil and natural gas has ensured that the oil-rich Gulf States and Algeria have the financial capability to procure large amounts of military hardware. Furthermore, within Latin America, these high oil prices have ensured that Venezuela has the financial capability to satisfy its arms requirements, with at least US$3 billion worth of arms contracts signed with Russia in the last four years, and more likely to follow. Such a large volume of arms will almost certainly upset the balance of power in Latin America,

---

3   Yasmann, 'Russia: Putin Pushes Greater Arms Exports'.
4   Richard Grimmett in 'Asia overtakes Middle East as developing world's arms market', 3 September 2005, available at <http://www.inq7.net>, accessed 22 February 2006.
5   Rosoboronexport Representative in, 'Russian Arms Exports up 15-Fold in Last Three Years—State Agency', 21 November 2005, available at <http://www.mosnews.com>, accessed 22 February 2006; and 'Ivanov says Russia's 2005 arms exports up 9% on year', available at <http://www.prime-tass.com>, accessed 6 March 2006.

and will probably trigger further sales to the region. In Southeast Asia, the traditional procurement of 'prestige pieces' of military hardware has resumed, following the recovery from the 1997–98 Asian financial economic crisis, and the subsequent growth in defence budgets.

Regional Sales Drives

The Middle East

Marketing arms to the conflict prone Middle East has never been particularly difficult for the world's arms exporters. However, the region's thirst for arms has been superseded in recent years by Asia, and market competition has ensured that Russian arms manufacturers have had to maintain a considerable sales drive within the Middle East.

The Middle East market includes states that have large debts to Russia, such as Libya and Syria. Others have important economic relations with Russia, such as Turkey and Iran. Of major importance to Russia are its relations with Turkey and Iran, particularly given their influence in Central Asia and Transcaucasia and the potential threat they pose to Russia's influence in those regions. In 2002, Turkey was the largest market for Russian exports in the Middle East, accounting for nearly 48 per cent of Russian exports to the region. Sales to Iran accounted for 11 per cent.[6] The Persian Gulf is also a Russian priority because the oil-rich states have the ability to pay. Moscow has sought, though not always successfully, to balance its policy among Iran and the Gulf Cooperation Council states. Russia operates in the Middle East within the context of its Soviet legacy, but it cannot afford to offer the subsidies that the Soviet Union bestowed or that the United States provides through its military aid to Israel, Egypt, and other regional allies. Nonetheless, Russia's newfound willingness to offer flexible finance may well support its position in Middle Eastern states such as Syria and Morocco, considered to be on the region's financial periphery.

Between 1992 and 2003, the Middle East was Russia's third largest market, after China and India, and was worth about US$10 billion in 2003 prices, equating to 17 per cent of its total arms exports. The largest purchaser within the Middle East was Iran (US$3.7 billion) followed by Algeria (US$2.3 billion) and the United Arab Emirates (UAE) (US$1.8 billion). Other significant markets were Yemen, Syria, Kuwait, Sudan, Egypt, and Turkey.[7] Between 1992 and 1999,

---

6   Paul Rivlin, *The Russian Economy and Arms Exports to the Middle East*, Memorandum no. 79, Jafee Center for Strategic Studies, Tel Aviv University, November 2005, p. 34, available at <http://www.inss.org.il/upload/(FILE)1188301974.pdf>, accessed 28 April 2009.
7   Rivlin, *The Russian Economy and Arms Exports to the Middle East*, p. 34.

Russian arms exports to the Middle East averaged about US$620 million a year. Between 1999 and 2003, they rose to nearly US$1.3 billion a year. The volume of Russian arms sales during this period was strongly influenced by the changing circumstances of each Middle East purchaser. As oil underpins most Middle Eastern economies, these changing conditions were largely due to fluctuating oil revenues, governed by changes in the price of oil. From 1992 until 1998, oil prices were weak; by 1998, oil prices had slumped to a low of about US$12 per barrel. Since then they have increased, and reached over US$140 per barrel in 2008. Predictably, therefore, arms sales share a positive correlation with the price of oil, which is likely to remain high for at least the next 25 years according to the International Energy Agency. Sales grew in the period from 1998, marked especially by purchases by Algeria, Iran, the UAE and Yemen.[8]

Sales to Iran and Syria are a politically sensitive issue for Russia because the United States perceives both states to be active supporters of terrorism. Russian sales have continued, however, as only weapons of a defensive nature are sold to these countries. 'Defensive' in this case is a somewhat loose term and over the last three years this has encompassed *Kornet* and *Metis* anti-tank guided weapons and *Igla* MANPADS to Syria and Su-25 *Frogfoot* close air support aircraft and *Tor* M1 (SA-15) air defence systems to Iran.[9] Interestingly, the *Kornet* and *Metis* systems were used to great effect by Hezbollah during the last Israeli incursion into Lebanon. Syria's facilitation of arms deliveries to Hezbollah may see stricter export controls being exercised by the Russians, but ongoing negotiations for the delivery of MiG-29 and Su-27 fighter aircraft will probably continue until an agreement is made, as Hezbollah cannot utilise these platforms. On the other hand, Iran's receipt of Russian weaponry looks set to continue. The Iranian Su-25 and *Tor* M1 contracts were signed in 2005, despite US protestations, and were the first arms agreements signed by both states since 2000, suggesting a renewal of the old relationship. Iran's interest in Russian S-300 long-range SAM systems, the upgrade of its *Kilo*-class submarines, and the past agreement with Russia in upgrading its Su-24 *Fencer* strike aircraft and T-72 MBT fleets, could see further sales, albeit under the watchful eye of the United States.

The two other key customers in the Middle East for Russia are Yemen and the UAE. Since 2002, Yemen and Russia have developed their relationship into that of traditional 'buyer–seller'. Yemen has procured 22 MiG-29 fighter aircraft, as well as 180 BMP-2 Infantry Fighting Vehicles (IFVs) since 2002, and future sales are almost certain, with a US$1.3 billion order for 32 of the advanced MiG-29SMT variants close to agreement. Like many of the global MiG-29 operators, Yemen

---

8   Rivlin, *The Russian Economy and Arms Exports to the Middle East*, p. 35.
9   Liam Devlin and Tom Cooper, 'Iran bolsters Su-25 fleet', *Jane's Defence Weekly*, 20 September 2006.

is also upgrading its older MiG-29 fleet to SMT standard which, according to MiG officials, boosts the aircraft's capability by more than 300 per cent, whilst reducing operating costs by 40 per cent.[10]

The UAE military relationship runs deeper than mere procurement, as the UAE is involved in funding Russian research and development (R&D). The UAE bought 402 BMP-3 IFVs from Russia between 1994 and 2000 and, more importantly, signed a contract for the development and exclusive delivery of the *Pantsyr*-S1 air defence system for US$500 million in mid-2000.[11] This capable system comprises both missile and gun armaments on a mobile platform and has the capacity to track and engage four air targets simultaneously.[12] To be delivered in 2009, the contract stipulates that the UAE and Russia will be the exclusive users for two years after the final delivery date. The systems manufacturer, KBP Tula, stated that it has concluded US$2.6 billion worth of contracts for the system,[13] presumably with the UAE and other countries prepared to wait two years for delivery. The UAE's relationship with Russia's OPK is important not only for financial return and R&D funding; it is also an example of the traditional Western arms procuring countries that have now begun to diversify and procure Russian equipment. A new contract between Russia and the UAE for shore-based *Klub* (SS-N-27 *Sizzler*) missile systems signed in Abu Dhabi in October 2006,[14] during Putin's visit, demonstrates the strength of the two states' burgeoning relationship.

The renewed Russian sales drive into the Middle East has been very fruitful due to the large number of Soviet and Russian sourced platforms in the region. Countries that operate such platforms include Algeria, Libya, Egypt, Syria, Yemen, the UAE and Iran, whilst traditional Western procuring countries such as Morocco, Kuwait and Saudi Arabia have begun to diversify by procuring niche Russian equipment such as air defence and multiple-launch rocket systems. This newfound interest in Russian weapons stems from a combination of competitively priced and durable products that in many cases have no Western analogue or equal. Morocco was looking to sign a US$1 billion arms deal with Russia following Putin's visit to Casablanca in September 2006. Although still undecided, the contract was expected to include Mi-17 helicopters, BMP-3 and BTR-90 vehicles, the *Metis* anti-tank guided missile system and a further

---

10   B. Vogel and P. Butowski, 'Yemen poised to order MiG 29SMTs', *Jane's Defence Weekly*, 13 September 2006.

11   Estimates put the cost at over US$800 million, as development was more expensive than was first anticipated.

12   M. Gyuros, 'Delays but increased capability for Pantsir', *Jane's Defence Weekly*, 16 August 2006.

13   'Russia Reports $2.6Bln Air Defense Sale Deal', 21 September 2006, available at <http://www.news-rus. com/2006/09/21/russia_reports_2_6bln_air_defense_sale_deal/>, accessed 28 April 2009.

14   Alexandra Gritskova and Konstantin Lantratov, 'Russian Rockets Will Keep Emirates Shores Safe', 23 August 2006, available at <http://www.kommersant.com/p699605/r_1/Russian_Rockets_Will_Keep_ Emirates_Shores_Safe/>, accessed 28 April 2009.

tranche of *Tunguska* air-defence systems.[15] It is likely that this as yet undecided deal is a direct response to Algeria's large arms contract signed in 2006 and it bodes well for future Russian sales to North Africa. Moreover, Russia agreed to cancel Libya's US$4.5 billion foreign debt in April 2008, paving the way for an arms and oil deal in similar structure to that of Algeria's before the end of 2008.[16]

Southeast Asia

Southeast Asia is another geographic region focusing on military modernisation. During the 1990s the bulk of the Association of Southeast Asian Nations (ASEAN) member states had ambitious programs for improving their armed forces capabilities. These programs were not merely responses to particular threats, but, for the most part, reflected long-established, domestically-based strategic rationales. These rationales included the increasing availability of funding, the military's role in decision-making, internal security concerns, overall national modernisation and industrialisation and supplier pressure/corruption.[17]

The Asian financial crisis which permeated through the region in 1997–98 reduced overall economic growth and cut state revenues, forcing several Southeast Asian governments to drastically curtail defence spending. At the same time, local currency depreciation against the dollar substantially reduced the international purchasing power of the remaining procurement funds. Most ASEAN member state economies have now recovered to pre-crisis levels and defence spending has resumed its pattern of growth in Indonesia, Thailand and Malaysia

Russia has been eager to exploit these newfound Southeast Asian fortunes by securing arms contracts. With only Vietnam a traditional user of its weaponry (Indonesia had transferred to Western-sourced equipment after Suharto came to power in the 1960s), Russia was almost entering an untried market. However, beginning with a delivery of MiG-29 fighter aircraft to Malaysia in 1993, and continuing after Putin's election as President in 1999, Russia made considerable inroads into the Southeast Asian arms market. Russian MiG-29 and Su-27/Su-30 combat aircraft are now present in the inventories of Myanmar, Malaysia, Indonesia and Vietnam; and Thailand may well follow suit, in a traditional response to growing military capabilities across its borders. Indeed, the total

---

15   Konstantin Lantratov, 'The Moroccan minister arrived in Moscow for weapons', *Kommersant*, Moscow, 9 June 2006, p. 10.

16   O. Shchedrov, 'Russia, Libya seal debt accord, eye arms deals', *Reuters*, Tripoli, 18 April 2008, available at   <http://www.polity.org.za/article/russia-libya-seal-debt-accord-eye-arms-deals-2008-04-18>,   accessed 28 April 2009.

17   Tim Huxley, 'Southeast Asian Force Modernisation', *Global Forces 2005: Proceedings of the ASPI conference. Day 2—Strategic Change*, Australian Strategic Policy Institute, Canberra, 2005, p. 46.

value of arms export contracts signed with Malaysia, Indonesia and Vietnam in 2003 exceeded that of arms export contracts signed with China or India, heralding Southeast Asia as a new major destination for Russian arms.[18]

Other than aircraft contracts, Vietnam and Singapore have received Russian air-defence systems, varying from the S-300 long-range unit to the *Igla* MANPADS. Myanmar and Malaysia are also considering contracts for medium-range systems. Traditionally, procurement of new capabilities in Southeast Asia has led other countries within the region to follow suit, such as the Singaporean submarine program being hotly followed by a Malaysian one. This would suggest that the aforementioned air-defence systems would spur other countries such as Indonesia and possibly Thailand to also embark upon improved air-defence programs of their own in an effort to keep up with the military developments of their neighbours—a trend that has occurred since the 1960s.

Russian naval exports to Southeast Asia have so far been exclusively to Vietnam; however Indonesia has ordered *Kilo*-class submarines within its US$1 billion export credit offer, and possibly a *Steregushchyy* frigate to be constructed in Spain as part of a separate deal.[19] Moreover, Vietnam's recent orders have been for 12 *Tarantul* fast-attack craft, two *Gepard* frigates, and interest has been shown for the *Steregushchyy* frigate: moves sure to spike the interest in the governments of the remaining Spratly Islands claimants, including those of the Philippines and Malaysia.[20] Both of these countries have been subjected to heavy marketing (Russia sent its largest naval exhibition to Malaysia's Langkawi-based biennial arms show—LIMA, in 2009) for Russian fast-attack vessels that are highly suited to operations in and around the Spratly Islands. Of course, other than regional one-upmanship and territorial disputes, there is the fact that China to the north and India to the west have devoted billions to their naval modernisation programs, which in turn has stimulated the requirement for naval vessels within Southeast Asia.

Latin America

The final corner of the Russian arms drive triangle is Latin America. Like Southeast Asia, this region has traditionally preferred Western-sourced equipment, but changing governments, aggressive US foreign policy and successful Russian marketing have seen many Latin American countries shift their procurement preference to Russian arms. Both Mexico and Uruguay have

---

18   'Russia—Tightening State Control', *East Asian Strategic Review 2005*, National Institute for Defense Studies, Tokyo, 2005, p. 184.

19   'Russia, Indonesia sign corvette construction agreement', *RIA Novosti*, 29 June 2007, available at <http://en.rian.ru/russia/20070629/68046148.html>, accessed 28 April 2009.

20   'Russian Weapons for Southeast Asia', *Kommersant*, 13 December 2005, available at <http://www.kommersant.com/p634447/r_500/Russian_Weapons_for_Southeast_Asia/>, accessed 28 April 2009.

bought small numbers of Russian weapon systems in recent years. Mexico purchased a fleet of Mi-17 helicopters, whilst Uruguay focused on land systems such as trucks and IFVs. However, two recent developments in Mexico are worthy of further mention. First, Rosoboronexport agreed to build a service centre for Russian equipment in Mexico in 2004, indicating the likelihood of future sales there. Indeed, a new contract was signed in June 2006 with the Mexican Navy selecting a fleet of 10 Su-27 fighters to form its first air defence unit.[21]

Further evidence of Russian expansion into the Latin American arms market came from the SINPRODE 2006 arms expo, held in Argentina in September 2006. Rosoboronexport sent its largest delegation to date and came away with a contract for the delivery of Mi-17 helicopters to the Chilean Army and Air force, and an agreement with Brazil to buy an unspecified model of the Sukhoi *Flanker* family of fighter aircraft.[22] The Mexican and Brazilian pilots of these Sukhoi aircraft will apparently be trained in Venezuela. Furthermore, the SINPRODE exhibition gave Rosoboronexport the opportunity to showcase a number of weapon systems it is hoping to export to Argentina as part of an 'arms for beef' deal. Russia is currently the largest importer of Argentine beef and, after the 2001 economic downturn in Argentina, the country could not fund its military procurement programs. Therefore, an 'arms for beef' barter deal was offered to Argentina. If Argentina agrees to the proposal, it could acquire *Tor* (SA-15), *Buk* (SA-11) or *Tunguska* (SA-19) air defence systems, Mi-35 attack helicopters, and unspecified number and class of naval craft as part of the contract. This offer follows on from an intergovernmental memorandum on military-technical cooperation signed in June 2004 and a presentation by Rosoboronexport to the Argentine military in 2005.[23]

By far the most important development within the Latin American market, however, has been Russia's courting of Venezuela. An agreement signed by Hugo Chavez and Vladimir Putin in Moscow in 2001 laid the framework for military cooperation and it bore fruit in 2005 with the signing of contracts for small arms, transport and attack helicopters. Future deliveries may include submarines and fighter aircraft, as Caracas moves steadily away from the US camp. The last two years have seen arms contracts valued at over US$3 billion signed between Caracas and Moscow, at a time when rhetoric and arms embargo have soured US-Venezuela relations to an all-time low. Russia has exploited the US arms embargo, which has prevented President Hugo Chavez from procuring US and European equipment with US-sourced components. In particular,

---

21   'Mexico: 10 Su-27s selected by Navy', *Military Procurement International*, Switzerland, 1 June 2006, p. 3.

22   'Russia to Sell Sukhoi Warplanes to Mexico, Brazil—State Arms Exporter', 28 September 2006, available at <http://www.mosnews.com>, accessed 30 September 2006.

23   'Russia offers Argentina e 'weapons for beef' barter deal', *Jane's Missiles and Rockets*, Jane's Information Group, Coulsdon, Surrey, 1 October 2006.

the embargo has led to the collapse of a Spanish contract to provide CN-235 transport aircraft with US components, and, for the same reason, could yet lead to a cancellation of a contract for Spanish built offshore patrol vessels. As the vast bulk of the Venezuelan military inventory is of US or European origin, Russia could yet gain even further arms contracts from Caracas. Contracts to date have included 100 000 AK-103 *Kalashnikov* derivative assault rifles, and an agreement to set up factories within Venezuela for their licence-production.[24] Moreover, the July 2006 visit by Chavez to Moscow yielded a contract for 30 Su-30MK2 multi-role fighters and 33 helicopters to add to the 15 Mi-17 utility, Mi-35 attack and Mi-26 heavy lift helicopters signed for in 2005.[25] Furthermore, the outcome of the July 2008 visit by Chavez to Moscow is a deal for an additional 12 Su-30MK2, expected to be signed before the end of the year.[26] These deals are no doubt partly responsible for the Mexican, Chilean and Brazilian decision to procure Russian equipment in response to Venezuela's arms purchases and will have an impact on the balance of power in Latin America.

More Venezuelan arms deals with Russia are likely to follow, as the country has an ambitious military modernisation program, considerable oil revenues with which to pay and few sourcing options due to US restrictions. The Venezuelan Navy requires a number of frigates and three submarines and *Jane's* sources in Venezuela indicated that the Russian *Amur*-class or *Kilo*-class diesel–electric submarine will be the preferred choice for the submarine requirement.[27] Furthermore, *Tor* M1 (SA-15) and S-300 (SA-10) air-defence systems are on the Venezuelan shopping list, with the total value of the armed forces modernisation program out to 2012 being some US$31 billion.[28] This is a considerable sum and its completion will be heavily reliant upon world oil prices remaining high. Even so, from the Russian perspective it is an encouraging development and one that will likely see further Russian arms deliveries not only to Venezuela but also to its regional neighbours, who will need to respond to Caracas' modernisation drive to remain militarily competitive.

---

24   'Chavez hails Russian arms deals', 27 July 2006, available at <http://news.bbc.co.uk/2/hi/europe/5221468.stm>, accessed 28 April 2009.

25   'Venezuela Reportedly Finalises $1B Deal for Helicopters, SU-30s', 27 July 2006, available at <http://www.defenseindustrydaily.com>, accessed 28 April 2009.

26   J. Higuera, 'Venezuela looks to Russia for new fighter, air defence *systems', Jane's Defence* Weekly, 1 August 2008.

27   J. Higuera, 'Russia poised to win Venezuelan contract', *Jane's Defence Weekly,* 14 June 2006.

28   'Venezuela Poised to Take Over as Top Latin American Buyer', 14 November 2005, Press Release, Forecast International, available at <http://www.forecastinternational.com/press/release.cfm?article=82>, accessed 28 April 2009.

Creative Export Practices

A key ingredient to the success in Russian arms export diversification has been a newfound willingness to accept flexible means of payment. The early 1990s saw barter trade with China as a component of its arms contracts, but Russian determination to earn hard currency ensured that barter trade only ever made up a percentage of an arms deal, never the total amount. Since 2000, efforts made by Putin and Ivanov have ensured that more diverse payment options are now available to Russia's arms customers. Moreover, the global boom in oil and natural gas prices has given the Russian Government a stronger financial position, negating the old desperation for hard currency. Moscow's flexibility has seen it explore finance options such as offsets, the clearing of Soviet-era foreign debt, and the offering of export credit to its arms customers.

As previously mentioned, Russia offered Indonesia an export credit for arms procurement in 2006. Interestingly, this was the first time Russia had offered its arms wholly on the basis of credit, indicating the strong desire to secure Indonesian business and the first example of a new arms export policy. The deal includes an offer of US$1 billion credit for the procurement of military equipment, to be paid back in two US$500 million installments over the next five years.[29] Indonesia has been interested in procuring Russian equipment such as the Su-30 *Flanker*, Russian *Steregushchyy* corvettes and submarines, but economic crises and natural disasters have continuously delayed government funding for such projects.[30] The offer of credit means Russia can secure Indonesian business earlier than would be the case under a conventional agreement, thereby ensuring that Indonesia becomes a major regional customer. The details of the package were confirmed following Putin's September 2007 visit to Jakarta, with 10 Mi-17 utility and five Mi-35 attack helicopters, 20 BMP-3 IFVs, two *Kilo* 636 submarines and a weapons package for the Su-27/30 *Flanker* fleet making up the costs.[31] Outside of the credit agreement, Indonesia ordered six more Su-27 *Flanker* aircraft at the MAKS 2007 airshow in Moscow; and in June 2007 signed a contract for the design and construction of corvettes based on the *Steregushchy*-class frigate.[32]

Myanmar is another likely recipient of Russian flexible finance in exchange for arms. Following an historic April 2006 visit by high-ranking Burmese military officials to Moscow, a Memorandum of Understanding (MoU) was

---

29   'Russia will arms Indonesia on credit', *Kommersant*, Moscow, 9 June 2006, p. 10.

30   'Exploring Russia, Forgetting Indonesia', *Tempo Magazine*, 13 October 2005, available at <http://www.antenna.nl/~amokmar/projecten/Indonesie/pers/Russia.html>, accessed 28 April 2009.

31   Donald Greenlees, 'Russia Widens Its Asian Reach With Arms Deals', *New York Times*, 6 September 2007, available at <http://www.nytimes.com/2007/09/06/world/asia/06indo.html?scp=5&sq=indonesia%20russia%202007&st=cse>, accessed 28 April 2009.

32   *RIA* Novosti, 2 July 2007.

signed between Russian oil giant Zaburezhneft and the Myanmar Ministry of Energy. The MoU included giving Russia access to the oil and gas fields in Myanmar. Several Russian media sources, including *RIA Novosti*, *Pravda* and *Kommersant*, suggested that this MoU was a means for Myanmar to repay Russia for a rumoured arms deal that also took place in April.[33] There is speculation that Myanmar may opt for MiG-29 fighters and either the *Tor* (SA-15) or *Buk* (SA-11) air-defence systems.[34] If true, it would imply that Russia is beginning to utilise an 'arms for oil' policy for its arms exports, because the Algerian contract signed a month earlier also incorporated an oil and gas component. Moreover, future arms deals with countries such as Malaysia, Vietnam, Indonesia and Venezuela may also include oil and gas components, as each of these countries has large reserves of one or both of these fossil fuels.

However, the attraction of Russian arms to these new markets is by no means restricted to financial benefit. Russian military equipment is perceived as durable and now includes a slowly improving after-sales service reputation. More importantly, these weapon systems go to countries such as Iran, India, China, Venezuela and Indonesia who do not fear a Russian embargo in response to political or human rights abuses. Russia's heedlessness to political factors, in conjunction with the aforementioned flexible finance policies, gives Russia, rather than the United States, preferred status as an arms supplier to these countries and to a growing number of other countries that are beginning to show a preference to the non-aligned camp.

The Algerian Deal: Russia's Largest

Like Myanmar, Algeria has allowed Russian access to its oil and gas deposits as part of an arms procurement package. The US$7.5 billion deal is the biggest single contract in the field of military-technical cooperation in Russian post-Soviet history.[35] It was signed in March 2006, during Putin's visit to Algiers, and includes a further US$2-3 billion option package for further arms. As Ruslan Pukhov, the Director of the Centre for Analysis of Strategies and Technologies, has stated: 'The contract will be Russia's triumphant return to North Africa … [And] the deal will trigger a pride race among the North African nations.'[36]

---

33   Dmitry Kosyrev, 'Myanmar: new field of Russia, China *Cooperation*', *RIA* Novosti, 5 April 2006, available at <http://www.news-rus.com/2006/04/05/myanmar_new_field_of_russia_china_cooperation/>, accessed 28 April 2009; and 'Foreign ministers of Russia, Myanmar meet in Moscow', 3 April 2006, available at <http://english.pravda.ru/news/world/03-04-2006/78266-%20Myanmar-0>, accessed 28 April 2009.

34   Guy Anderson, 'Russia eyes arms for energy deal with Myanmar', *Jane's Defence Weekly*, 12 April 2006.

35   'Putin rates highly results of his 'lightning visit' to Algeria', *Moscow Rossiyskaya Gazeta*, Moscow, 11 March 2006.

36   Ruslan Pukhov, in an interview conducted at the Centre for Analysis of Strategies and Technologies, Moscow, 6 June 2006, and Ruslan Pukhov, in Nabi Abdullaev, 'Russia eyes debt-for-deals strategy', 20 March 2006, available at <http://www.cast.ru/eng/?id=231>, accessed 28 April 2009.

The US$7.5 billion deal for arms signed with Algeria in March 2006 included the suspension of Algeria's US$4.7 billion Soviet-era foreign debt, and this action could trigger further arms for debt suspension deals in the region, with Libya and Syria also being recipients of Soviet-era loans. Therefore, one of the important factors impinging upon the Algerian deal is the response it may trigger from Morocco, Libya and Egypt, who are all currently discussing arms packages of varying size with the Russians. This will ensure that the North African market takes some of the strain from the projected downturn in arms transfers to China. The other important factor is the way the deal was structured. Like many Russian arms deals, only some of the specific details have been disclosed to the public. What is known, however, is that it includes the writing-off of US$4.7 billion worth of Soviet-era foreign debt and that this was the key component of the deal that ensured Algerian agreement to take the Russian arms package. Furthermore, Algeria extracted from Russia an assurance that Moscow would not object to Algeria's early payment of its US$8 billion debt to the Paris Club.[37]

Other than the above concessions, Algeria is to receive a US$3.5 billion air package, including 34 MiG-29SMT fighters, 28 Su-30MKA fighters, and 14 *Yak*-130 advanced jet trainers between now and 2009. A US$2-3 billion option package was also signed and, if Algeria exercises these options, it is predicted that it will receive a further 20 MiG-29SMTs and 16 *Yak*-130s.[38] Coupled with the original deal is a ground package of *Metis* and *Kornet* anti-tank guided missiles, 180 T-90S MBTs, the upgrade of 250 T-72 MBTs, and an air defence package of 30 *Tunguska* (SA-19) and eight batteries of S-300 (SA-10) air-defence systems.[39] This ground component is worth in excess of US$2 billion. The contract also includes unspecified work on various Algerian naval vessels. Furthermore, Algeria has agreed to part with another US$400 million as part of a separate contract for two more *Kilo*-class submarines, signed in June 2006. Clearly, Algeria is undertaking a near total refurbishment of its largely Cold War era armed forces including naval, ground and air components, and Russia is the facilitator.

---

37   Andrei Maslov, 'Risk Factors of the Delivery of Russian Arms to Algeria', *Moscow Defense Brief*, Issue 2, 2006, available at <http://mdb.cast.ru/mdb/2-2006/item3/item2/>, accessed 28 April 2009. The Paris Club (and thus the name) arose out of crisis talks that were held in Paris in 1956 between Argentina and its various creditors. It is an informal group of financial officials from 19 countries, with the current permanent member-nations being: Australia, Austria, Belgium, Canada, Denmark, Finland, France, Germany, Ireland, Italy, Japan, the Netherlands, Norway, Russia, Spain, Sweden, Switzerland, United Kingdom, and the United States.
38   Konstantin Makienko and Dmitry Vasiliev, 'The Algerian Deal', *Moscow Defense Brief*, Issue 2, 2006, available at <http://mdb.cast.ru/mdb/2-2006/item3/item1/>, accessed 28 April 2009.
39   'Algerian Arms Deal Brings Russia US$7.5 billion, Gas Market Leverage', 15 March 2006, available at <http://www.defenseindustrydaily.com/algerian-arms-deal-brings-russia-75-billion-gas-market-leverage-02024/>, accessed 28 April 2009.

Russia receives three major returns in its structuring of the Algerian deal. First, it has probably gained access to Algeria's oil and gas fields. Accompanying Putin on his Algiers visit were the heads of Gazprom, Lukoil and Itera—three of Russia's largest oil and gas companies.[40] Despite few official statements from either government, the presence of the gas and oil chiefs and a subsequent MoU signed between Algerian gas giant Sonatrach and Gazprom in August 2006[41] indicate a developing relationship within the oil and gas sector. The final arrangement is that Algiers will probably give those Russian oil and gas companies access to Algerian deposits, with the proceeds split between the producers and the Algerian Government.[42] The Algerian Government is then bound to immediately transfer the revenues to Russian arms manufacturers until such time as the debt is paid off. Moreover, Algeria will also share its expertise in gas liquefaction (a legacy of French rule and subsequent investment), and Sonatrach has already promised to help build infrastructure for the production of liquefied natural gas in Russia.[43] Despite Russia's huge natural gas reserves, its knowledge and experience in gas liquefaction remains relatively limited compared to the West and Sonatrach will help to rectify these deficiencies within the Russian gas fields.

The second return Russia will receive from the Algerian deal is yet another boost to the OPK, with more concrete orders ensuring continued work and finance for several weapons production lines. It has given RSK MiG valuable orders, which will assist the company in its quest to gain the lucrative US$5-9 billion contract for India's 126 Medium Multi-role Combat Aircraft tender. The Algerian deal also gave Yakovlev its first export customer for the *Yak*-130 advanced jet trainer, necessitating the opening of a second production line for the aircraft. As important, the deal touched every facet of the Russian OPK: aerospace, naval and ground—something very rare in terms of arms contracts, which are not normally so universal and usually only favour one of the three sectors.

Finally, both Ivan Safranchuk (the head of the Moscow branch of the Centre for Defence Information) and Ruslan Pukhov concurred that the Algerian deal will bring further regional orders for Russian arms because of the impact the deal will have on the balance of power in North Africa. The next most likely customers for a 'debt for arms' swap are Libya and, to a lesser extent, Egypt and Morocco, because of their close proximity to Algeria, possession of Soviet-era

---

40   Nabi Abdullaev, 'Russia eyes debt-for-deals strategy', *Defense News,* 20 March 2006, available at <http://www.cast.ru/eng/comments/?id=231>, accessed 28 April 2009.
41   'Gazprom, Algeria's Sonatrach Sign Official Cooperation Accord', 14 August 2006, available at <http://www.mosnews.com>, accessed 8 October 2006.
42   'Algerian Arms Deal Brings Russia US$7.5 billion, Gas Market Leverage', 15 March 2006.
43   'Algeria signs $5 billion arms-for-energy deal with Russia', *Military Procurement International,* vol. 16, no. 6, 15 April 2006, p. 1.

foreign debt, and largely Russian sourced weapon systems. Libya in particular is likely to be Russia's next major North African arms customer, as it has large gas and oil deposits, an outdated military, and a recently forgiven US$4.3 billion Soviet-era foreign debt to Moscow.

Arms Market Diversification: A Return to Soviet Policy?

Russia's newfound willingness to accept recompense other than hard currency for its military hardware is clearly apparent. However, the reasoning behind such a policy shift remains a mystery. There is no doubt that that arms-market diversification has assisted Russia's OPK with more weapons orders, but the meshing of energy sector agreements with arms agreements, export credits, and the growing use of Russian weapon systems around the globe is also contributing to Russia's growing political influence.

During the Cold War, the Soviet Union and the United States used arms transfers and military assistance as one element in foreign and security policies that was primarily intended to further a political and ideological competition.[44] The traditional arms clients of the former Soviet Union were more often than not poorer developing countries valued more for their ideological tendencies and desire for Soviet weaponry, rather than for their financial credentials. Today, Russia's arms exports to Myanmar in exchange for oil concessions and Indonesia for export credit are reminiscent of the deals struck with the developing countries during the Soviet era. Many of the Soviet client-states received substantial military aid grants and significant discounts on their arms purchases, although this trend is yet to appear within current Russian arms exports.

Russia's regional sales drive is proof that arms exports are no longer just about receiving hard currency. Argentina's potential 'arms for beef' deal, Algeria's debt reduction and 'arms for oil' deal, Burma's likely 'arms for oil' deal and Indonesia's export credit all offer concrete examples of the Russian policy change. Whether or not political considerations or energy politics are at play when Russia decides upon new arms contracts remains unclear; however the thirst for hard currency has certainly been quenched since those anxious years following the collapse of the Soviet Union. What is clear is that the increasingly concerted effort by Russia to cast it arms out to a wider net, in anticipation of an eventual Chinese market closure, is proving to be of great assistance to the longevity and success of the Russian OPK.

---

44   See press release for Ian Anthony (ed.), *Russia and the Arms Trade,* available at <http://editors.sipri.se/pubs/pressre/iabk2.html>, accessed 28 April 2009.

Chapter 7
Conclusion

Russia's *Oboronnyi-promyshennyi kompleks* (OPK) has embarked on a pathway to recovery and resurgence. It has emerged from its bleak post-Soviet reputation as a fragmented and disintegrating behemoth into a more streamlined, centrally controlled institution worthy of its status as one of the world's most prominent arms suppliers. Whilst the OPK's long-term success is far from assured, the doubts surrounding its continued existence have quickly dissolved as its economic position has gone from strength to strength. Reliable economic links have been forged with India and China through regular military orders and the emerging markets that Rosoboronexport has fought hard to cultivate in Latin America, the Middle East and Southeast Asia are all beginning to pay dividends.

Domestically, the key drivers required for the OPK are all underway in some capacity. The Russian Government has finally realised the importance of linking OPK restructure with military reform. State structures and new Commissions, such as the Military Industrial Commission chaired by former Defence Minister Sergei Ivanov, are now coming into play and will greatly assist the required linkage. Corruption remains endemic, but a more aggressive government approach to kerbing it, through high profile arrests and the introduction of Western auditors, are proof that the issue is being taken seriously. Restructuring the OPK is also well underway, with the government pushing for greater state control, and the creation of large, sector specific conglomerates such as *Obyedinyonnaya Aviasroitelnaya Korporatsiya* (OAK). Finally, the urgent requirement for larger domestic orders is also being tackled, with the State Defence Order (SDO) finally devoting the bulk of its finances towards equipment replacement or refurbishment. It is too early to say whether or not the long-term success of the OPK is assured, but the domestic drivers that are required for this are all currently being implemented or built upon.

The external drivers have all been implemented and the OPK will continue to benefit from the Russian Government's efforts at consolidation in this field. China remains an important external driver due to its unquenchable desire for military capability and expansion. However, Russia remains savvy to the inherent economic and strategic risks associated with over-reliance upon the Chinese market. These factors, in conjunction with greater Chinese military self-reliance past 2012, suggest that the Chinese market will contract after this timeframe. In the meantime, however, it will remain a valuable customer.

India shares a more intimate relationship with Russia than does China, and this factor is shaping the growing military ties between the two countries. A similar strategic footing, Russian technical input and joint ventures, and heavy Indian reliance upon Russian weapon systems are the major tenets that shape Indo-Russian relations. These tenets will ensure that India remains the key Russian weapons customer in the long-term.

The growth in arms sales to Russia's emerging markets is irrefutable. The multi-billion dollar deals struck between 2006 and 2008 have the real potential to alter regional balances of power, and in turn generate further sales. This bodes well for the OPK, but the dynamics of the arms deals are generating questions about Russian motives. The more generous terms offered to Indonesia, the oil components of the arms deal with Algeria and Myanmar and the possible beef barter deal with Argentina are all indicators of a Russian policy change, because the constant in all previous arms deals since 1991—large cash components—are no longer a feature of these arms deals. However, regardless of Russian motives, the advances in exports are most beneficial to the OPK.

The final link will be complementing these export initiatives with more robust domestic demand. Here, Putin's plan to invest in R&D, and subsequently to modernise the armed forces, is beginning to bear early fruit, as indicated by the rapidly rising SDO figures.

Over the next decade it will be interesting to observe the OPK's ongoing development and market diversification in the face of Chinese indigenous competition and Russian domestic influences. It would be premature to suggest that the future of the OPK is assured. The new export opportunities will need to be consolidated. It will also be important for President Dmitry Medvedev and Defence Minister Anatoliy Serdyukov to continue the strong commitment shown by their predecessors towards the OPK's future development. A change of leadership policy, or problems with pushing through the reforms could arise. However, the diversity of the market and the emerging domestic demand suggest that the OPK is likely to endure and probably prosper beyond the next decade. At the close of 2008, the Russian Defence Industrial Complex stood at the cusp of greatness—an unimaginable prospect in 1998. It may just become the 'phoenix from the ashes'.

Selected Bibliography

Books

Agursky, Mikhail, *The Soviet Military Industrial Complex*, The Magnes Press, Jerusalem, 1980.

Aldis, Anne C., and Roger N. McDermott (eds), *Russian Military Reform 1992–2002*, Frank Cass, London, 2003.

Anthony, Ian (ed.), *Russia and the Arms Trade*, SIPRI, Oxford University Press, Oxford, 1998.

Baker, Peter, and Susan Glasser, *Kremlin Rising*, Scribner, New York, 2005.

Blank, Stephen J., *Reform and the Revolution in Russian Defense Economics*, Strategic Studies Institute, US Army War College, Carlisle, PA, 1995.

Conley, Jerome, *Indo-Russian Military and Nuclear Cooperation*, Lexington Books, Lanham, MD, 2001.

Cordesman, Anthony H., *The Strategic Impact of Russian Arms Sales and Technology Transfers*, Center for Strategic and International Studies, Washington, DC, 1999.

Gaddy, Clifford, *The Price of the Past: Russia's Struggle with the Legacy of a Militarized Economy*, Brookings Institution Press, Washington, DC, 1996.

Herspring, Dale R. (ed.), *Putin's Russia: Past Imperfect, Future Uncertain*, Rowman and Littlefield, Maryland, 2005.

Malleret, Thierry, *Conversion of the Defense Industry in the Former Soviet Union*, Institute for East-West Security Studies, Westview Press, New York, 1992.

Miller, Steven E., and Dmitri V. Trenin (eds), *The Russian Military: Power and Policy*, MIT Press, Cambridge, MA, 2004.

Pierre, Andrew J., and Dmitri V. Trenin (eds), *Russia in the World Arms Trade*, Carnegie Endowment for International Peace, Washington, DC, 1997.

Rosefielde, Steven, *Russia in the 21st Century*, Cambridge University Press, Cambridge, 2005.

Sergounin, Alexander A., and Sergey V. Subbotin, *Russian Arms Transfers to East Asia in the 1990s*, SIPRI Research Report no. 15, Oxford University Press, Oxford, 1999.

Tsai, Ming-Yen, *From Adversaries to Partners? Chinese and Russian Military Cooperation after the Cold War*, Praeger Publishers, Westport, CT, 2003.

Interviews and Speeches

Belova, Olga, (Television Presenter), in 'Segodnya', *Moscow NTV MIR*, 1000 GMT, 9 November 2005.

Donaldson, Robert H., 'Domestic influences on the Russian arms sale policy' Presented to the 43rd Annual Meeting of the International Studies Association, New Orleans, 2002.

Huxley, Tim, 'Southeast Asian Force Modernisation', *Global Forces 2005: Proceedings of the ASPI conference. Day 2—Strategic Change*, Canberra, 2005.

Pukhov, Ruslan, interview conducted at the Centre for Analysis of Strategies and Technologies, Moscow, 6 June 2006.

Newspapers

Baluyevskiy, Yuri, 'Igor Baluyevskiy: We do not intend waging war with NATO', *Moscow Rossiyskaya Gazeta*, Moscow, November 2005.

Dimitryev, I., 'Hello to Arms', *Versiya*, No. 19, 22–28 May 2006.

Gritskova, Alexandra, and Konstantin Lantratov, 'Russian Mi-17 to land in India', *Kommersant*, 11 July 2006.

Lantratov, Konstantin, 'The Moroccan minister arrived in Moscow for weapons', *Kommersant*, Moscow, 9 June 2006.

'Putin rates highly results of his 'lightning visit' to Algeria', Moscow *Rossiyskaya Gazeta*, Moscow, 11 March 2006.

'Russia will arms Indonesia on credit', *Kommersant*, Moscow, 9 June 2006.

Saranov, Vadim, 'Generals of the air force enrich themselves', *Versiya*, Moscow, 25 October 2004.

Journals, Magazines and Publications

'Algeria signs $5 billion arms-for-energy deal with Russia', *Military Procurement International*, vol. 16, no. 6, 15 April 2006.

Anderson, Guy, 'Russia eyes arms for energy deal with Myanmar', *Jane's Defence Weekly*, 12 April 2006.

Azizian, Rouben, 'Russia-India Relations: Stability amidst Strategic Uncertainty', *Special Assessment: Asia's Bilateral Relations*, Asia-Pacific Center for Security Studies, Honolulu, 2004.

Bedi, Rahul, 'India, Russia to renew accord for 10 more years', *Jane's Defence Weekly*, 30 November 2005.

Bonsignore, Luca, 'The Future of Rosoboronexport', *NATO's Nations and Partners for Peace*, vol. 49, no. 1, 2004.

Bouldin, Matthew, 'The Ivanov Doctrine and Military Reform: Reasserting Stability in Russia', *Journal of Slavic Military Studies*, vol. 17, no. 4, 2004.

Chemezov, Sergei, 'This is Rosoboronexport', *Military Technology*, vol. 28, no. 9, September 2004.

'China to buy 540t Zubr class assault hovercraft', *Military Procurement International*, vol. 16, no. 19, 1 October 2006.

'China's Confident Bow; China's increase in defence spending', *The Economist*, 10 March 2001.

de Haas, Marcel, 'Russian-Chinese military exercises and their wider perspective: Power play in Central Asia', Conflict Studies and Research Centre, Defence Academy of the United Kingdom, 2005.

'Defence Production and R&D', *Jane's Sentinel Security Assessment: Russia*, Jane's Information Group, Coulsdon, Surrey, September 2005.

'Defense Industry Complex: Punish or Pardon? Does the State need Wings?', *Ekonomicheskiye Strategii*, Moscow, 24 February 2005.

Devlin, Liam, and Tom Cooper, 'Iran bolsters Su-25 fleet', *Jane's Defence Weekly*, 20 September 2006.

Felgenhauer, Pavel, 'Arms Exports and the Russian Military', *Perspective*, vol. XII, no. 4, March–April 2002.

Galeotti, Mark and Ian M. Synge, 'Russia's Economy—The Best Case', *Putin's Russia—Scenarios for 2005*, Jane's Information Group, Coulsdon, Surrey, 2005.

Gertsev, O., 'Five Years of Rosoboronexport: Trends and Prospects', *Moscow Voyenno-Promyshlennyy*, Moscow, 26 October 2005.

Gill, Bates, 'China's Newest Warships', *Far Eastern Economic Review*, 27 January 2000.

Grimmett, Richard F., *Conventional Arms Transfers to Developing Nations, 1997–2004* Congressional Research Service, The Library of Congress, Washington, DC, 2005.

Gyuros, M., 'Delays but increased capability for Pantsir', *Jane's Defence Weekly*, 16 August 2006.

Herspring, Dale R., 'Vladimir Putin and Military Reform in Russia', *European Security*, vol. 14, no. 1, March 2005.

Higuera, J., 'Russia poised to win Venezuelan contract', *Jane's Defence Weekly*, 14 June 2006.

Isakova, Irina, *Russian Defense Reform: Current Trends*, Strategic Studies Institute, US Army War College, Carlisle, PA, November 2006.

Ivanov, Henry, 'Country Briefing: RUSSIA—Austere deterrence', *Jane's Defence Weekly*, 3 May 2006.

———, 'Russia details weapon procurement plans for 2006', *Jane's Defence Weekly*, London, November 2005.

Izyumov, Alexei, Leonid Kosals, Rosalina Ryvinka, and Yuri Semagin, 'Market Reforms and Regional Differentiation of Russia Defence Industry Enterprises', *Europe-Asia Studies*, vol. 54, no. 6, September 2002.

Jain, B.M., 'India and Russia: Reassessing the time tested ties', *Pacific Affairs*, vol. 76, no. 3, Fall 2003.

Jane's Ground Based Air Defence, Jane's Information Group, Coulsdon, Surrey, 2006.

Karniol, Robert A., 'Russian industry hunts out a future for itself', *Jane's Defence Weekly*, 1 March 2000.

Lansford, Tom, 'US-Russian Rivalry in the Arms Trade of South Asia', *Security Dialogue*, vol. 33, no. 2, June 2002.

Mahmud, Benjamin, 'Russian Defence Industry', *Asia Defence Journal*, October 2005.

'Mexico: 10 Su-27s selected by Navy', Military Procurement International, Switzerland, 1 June 2006.

Murphy, James, 'Putin moves to allay fears over EADS share buy', *Jane's Defence Weekly*, 4 October 2006.

———, 'Russia to Increase Defence Spending Following Challenging Period for Defence Industry', *Jane's Defence Industry*, 1 October 2005.

———, 'Russian Defence Exports Decline', *Jane's Defence Weekly*, 7 December 2005.

Novichkov, Nikolai, 'Rosoboronexport builds up its military exports', *Defense Technologies*, vol. 5, no. 2, Russian Defence Systems Publishers, Moscow, 2006.

———, 'Russian defence exports surpass targets', *Jane's Defence Industry*, 1 March 2006.

'Procurement', *Jane's Sentinel Security Assessment: Russia*, Jane's Information Group, Coulsdon, Surrey, March 2006.

Rivlin, Paul, *The Russian Economy and Arms Exports to the Middle East*, Memorandum no. 79, The Jaffee Centre for Strategic Studies, Tel Aviv University, 2005.

'Russia Aims to Make its MiG-35 Fighter the Pinnacle of 'Fulcrum' Development', *Jane's International Defence Review*, 1 January 2006.

'Russia offers Argentina 'weapons for beef' barter deal', *Jane's Missiles and Rockets*, Jane's Information Group, Coulsdon, Surrey, 1 October 2006.

'Russia—Tightening State Control', *East Asian Strategic Review 2005*, National Institute for Defense Studies, Tokyo, 2005.

Sánchez-Andrés, Antonio, 'Arms Exports and Restructuring in the Russian Defence Industry', *Europe-Asia Studies*, vol. 56, no. 5, July 2004.

SIPRI Yearbook 2006, Stockholm International Peace Research Institute, Oxford University Press, Oxford, 2006.

The Military Balance 2005, International Institute for Strategic Studies, Oxford University Press, Oxford, 2004.

The Military Balance 2006, International Institute for Strategic Studies, Oxford University Press, Oxford, 2006.

Vogel, B., and P. Butowski, 'Yemen poised to order MiG 29SMTs', *Jane's Defence Weekly*, 13 September 2006.

Websites

Asia Times newspaper: <www.atimes.com>

Axis Information and Analysis: <www.axisglobe.com>

BBC News: <news.bbc.co.uk>

Business Week: <www.businessweek.com>

Carnegie Endowment for International Peace: <www.carnegie.ru>

(Moscow Centre)

Cato Institute: <www.cato.org>

Christian Science Monitor: <www.csmonitor.com>

Defense Industry Daily: <www.defenseindustrydaily.com>

Defense News: <www.defensenews.com>

Economist: <www.economist.com>

Forecast International: <www.forecastinternational.com/>

Global Security: <www.globalsecurity.org>

Heritage Foundation: <www.heritage.org>

India Daily newspaper: <www.indiadaily.com>

Indian defence website: <www.india-defence.com>

Indian Ministry of Defence: <mod.nic.in>

Interfax Information Group: <www.interfax.com>

International Energy Agency: <www.iea.org>

Jane's Information Group: <www.janes.com/>

Kommersant newspaper: <www.kommersant.com>

Library of Congress, Federal Research Division: </lcweb2.loc.gov>

Moscow Defense Brief: <mdb.cast.ru>

Moscow News newspaper: <www.mosnews.com>

Pravda newspaper: <www.pravda.ru>

Prime Tass Business News Agency: <www.prime-tass.com>

RIA Novosti News Wire Service: <en.rian.ru>

Russia Journal: <beta.russiajournal.com>

Sovereign Publications: <www.sovereign-publications.com>

The World Today: <www.chathamhouse.org.uk/publications/twt/>
    (Chatham House)

Times newspaper: <www.timesonline.co.uk/tol/news/>

US Department of Defense: <www.defenselink.mil>

Website of the President of the Russian Federation: <www.kremlin.ru>

Wikipedia internet encyclopaedia: <en.wikipedia.org>

Glossary

Akula	Capable Soviet-era nuclear attack submarine. The Indian Navy is acquiring two refurbished hulls from the Russian Navy under a lease contract
Baltiysky Zavod	Baltic Shipyards, St. Petersburg
BMP-1/2/3	Russia's primary tracked Infantry Fighting Vehicle family
Buk SA-11	Medium-range air defence system also known as SA-11, and accommodating the *Gadfly* or *Grizzly* missile
Goskomstat	The Soviet state statistical agency
Gosplan	The Soviet state central planning agency
Irkut	Irkutsk based company and production facility for advanced variants of the Su-30 aircraft
KBP Tula	Tula based company specialising in the construction of armoured vehicles
Klub	A submarine-based fire-control system that includes the potent 3M-14 series missile, also known as the SS-N-27 *Sizzler*
KnAAPO	Komsomolsk-na-Amur based company and production facility for relatively advanced and base variants of the Su-27/30 aircraft
MiG	Mikoyan-im-Gureyevich, company specialising in the construction of combat aircraft
MiG-AT	Advanced trainer built with French collaboration
MiG-29 *Fulcrum*	1970s-era multi-role fighter aircraft that has seen prolific export and a series of upgrade programs (including MiG-29 SMT) maintaining its combat capabilities into the twenty-first century
MiG-35 *Fulcrum*	The pinnacle of *Fulcrum* development, currently being offered to India
OPK	*Oboronnyi-promyshennyi kompleks* (defence-industrial complex) is Russia's renamed VPK (military-industrial complex)
Pechora SA-3	Extensive upgrade package for the ageing S-125 SA-3 *Goa* SAM system
Project 677 *Amur*	Latest generation single hulled diesel-electric submarine, also known as *Lada*
Project 877/636 *Kilo*	Upgradeable 1980s-era double-hulled diesel-electric submarine
S-300 SA-10/20	Long range air defence system capable of accommodating the *Grumble* and *Gargoyle* family of missiles
SDO	State Defence Order: The allocation of budget funds to military procurement and research and development
Severnaya Verf	Russia's primary shipyards in St. Petersburg and producer of *Kilo*-class submarines
Stereguschyy	New generation of light frigate incorporating radar absorption technologies. Large export sales expected
Sukhoi	Russian aircraft design bureau, now conglomerated with production facilities
Su-24 *Fencer*	Sukhoi designed, 1970s-era deep penetration strike aircraft
Su-27/30 *Flanker*	Sukhoi designed 1980s-era air superiority and now multi-role combat aircraft. Widely exported and respected

Sovremennyy	Potent Russian destroyer designed to combat US carrier battle groups during the Cold War. Exported to China
T-72/80/90	Russia's main battle tank family, of which the T-72 and T-90 are still in production
Talwar	Advanced frigate based on the Soviet-era Krivak hull and built in Russia exclusively for the Indian Navy
Tor SA-15	Potent short-range high-altitude Russian air defence system also known as the SA-15, and accommodating the *Gauntlet* missile
Tupolev	Soviet-era aircraft design bureau focusing chiefly on bomber development
Uralvagonzavod	Ural's based company specialising in the construction of armoured vehicles
VPK	*Voennyi-promyshlennyi kompleks* (military-industrial complex) was a formal institutional network connecting the Soviet General Staff, Ministry of Defence, military enterprises, civilian firms, and construction, communications, planning, civil defence, military intelligence and other security organisations into a cohesive structurally militarised entity. The integration of the VPK is higher than its US counterpart, which is based on a loose community of interest
Yakovlev	Soviet-era aircraft design bureau
Yak-130	Russia's new generation advanced combat trainer, also known as *Mitten*
Yantar	Kaliningrad based Russian shipyard recently awarded with a contract to build three *Talwar* frigates for the Indian Navy

Index